STOKER MUNRO SURVIVOR

STOKER MUNRO SURVIVOR

DAVID SPITERI

HarperCollins*Publishers*

HarperCollins*Publishers*

First published in Australia in 2014
by HarperCollins*Publishers* Australia Pty Limited
ABN 36 009 913 517
harpercollins.com.au

HarperCollins*Publishers*
Level 13, 201 Elizabeth Street, Sydney NSW 2000, Australia
Unit D1, 63 Apollo Drive, Rosedale, Auckland 0632, New Zealand
A 53, Sector 57, Noida, UP, India
77–85 Fulham Palace Road, London W6 8JB, United Kingdom
2 Bloor Street East, 20th floor, Toronto, Ontario M4W 1A8, Canada
195 Broadway, New York, NY 10007, USA

National Library of Australia Cataloguing-in-Publication entry:

Spiteri, David, author.
  Stoker Munro: survivor / David Spiteri.
  978 0 7322 9891 3 (paperback)
  978 1 4607 0254 3 (ebook)
  Munro, Stoker.
  Changi POW Camp (Changi, Singapore) – Biography.
  Burma-Siam Railroad.
  World War, 1939-1945 – Personal narratives, Australian
  World War, 1939-1945 – Naval operations, Australian.
  World War, 1939-1945 – Prisoners and prisons,
  Japanese – Biography.
  World War, 1939-1945 – Prisoners and prisons,
  Australian – Biography.
  Prisoners of war – Australia – Biography.
940.547252

Cover design by Philip Campbell Design
Cover image: Stoker Lloyd 'Darby' Munro, supplied by the author
Maps by mapillustrations.com.au
Typeset in 11/16.5 Baskerville BE by Kirby Jones
Printed and bound in Australia by Griffin Press
The papers used by HarperCollins in the manufacture of this book
are a natural, recyclable product made from wood grown in sustainable
plantation forests. The fibre source and manufacturing processes meet
recognised international environmental standards, and carry certification.
Printed and bound in Australia by Griffin Press

5 4 3 2 1   14 15 16 17

For the descendants, Australian and American,

of the Java Rabble

Foreword by Mike Carlton

The men who went to war in the light cruiser HMAS *Perth* were part of a remarkable generation of Australians. Perhaps our greatest generation.

Growing up, they had lived through the hardship of the great Depression of the early 1930s. They knew poverty: what it was for a family to go hungry at night; or the absence of a father gone to look for work; or the sorrow of a mother pawning her wedding ring.

They did not complain. That's just how life was. Then, after the Depression lifted and times began to pick up, along came Hitler and Mussolini and the Second World War, just in time to catch this generation on the edge of adulthood.

Again they did not complain. They joined up to fight, not for flag-waving notions of King, Empire and Country, but because they had homes and families to defend. This motive, heartfelt, grew stronger and more visceral as the Japanese threat moved towards Australia in late 1941.

Few of *Perth*'s crew were professional sailors, men who had sought a career in the navy. Some of the senior men were experienced seamen who had joined in peacetime. Others had been reservists, mucking around in gigs and whalers to earn a few bob at weekends. But most were raw recruits, unfamiliar with the sea and its ways, and still less aware of the perils and horrors of naval warfare. It is to their immortal credit that they met those dangers with unflinching resolve and courage.

Lloyd William Munro was one of those fresh-faced youngsters, a kid from Byron Bay on the NSW north coast. Mobilised for service by proclamation, as the navy called it, he reported for duty on the 27th of February, 1941, just over a month after his seventeenth birthday. He was listed as a Stoker Class III, the very bottom rung of the ladder – literally, in his case, for his job would be far below decks in the engine room or boiler spaces, the very bowels of any ship that carried him to sea. The navy – always quick to bestow a nickname – inevitably called him 'Darby', after David 'Darby' Munro, the most famous jockey of the day.

Perth was his first and only ship in the war, and he was with her when she died. It was just past midnight, the morning of Sunday the 1st of March, 1942. After a fight of quite extraordinary gallantry, *Perth* and the American heavy cruiser USS *Houston* were sunk by an overwhelming Japanese force in the Sunda Strait that separates the islands of Java and Sumatra.

The story of Darby Munro's survival is an epic of the human spirit. David Spiteri – a sailor himself – has told it beautifully, with admiration and affection. In our time, when the word 'hero' is flung around so lightly, this book reflects upon genuine heroism. We forget these stories and these lives at our peril.

Mike Carlton
Author of *Cruiser, the Life and Loss of HMAS* Perth *and Her Crew*

Maps

List of illustrations

Prologue

I first met Stoker Munro over 25 years ago at the Byron Bay bowling club in northern New South Wales, after I had retired from the Royal Australian Navy. I'd heard he had also served in the navy but that was about all I knew. After almost twelve years of occasionally chatting over a beer, one day the HMAS *Perth* was mentioned and Stoker told me he had served on her. The penny never dropped for me as to what that meant coming from someone his age, but I did tell him I had also served on the *Perth* for four years and had an old *Perth* sailor's cap tally band at home. Would he like it? In his dry voice he just said, 'Yeah, I lost my last one.'

That afternoon a mutual friend, Nick Casey, said to me, 'You don't know Stoker's story, do you?'

'No,' I said. 'Can you tell me?'

I couldn't believe what I heard and immediately thought that I would love to re-tell the retiring man's story. Stoker wasn't interested, plus I was writing another book at the time, so I left it at that. When my book *The Prez* was published a while later I approached him again. I told him I didn't want to portray him as a hero but that his story deserved to be told, to inspire a younger generation to never give up no matter what barriers may be thrown up against them. I must have worn him down because eventually he started to relate little things; even after 60 years his memory remained vivid, and at times no detail was too small. He always took a back seat to the events he described and was blessed with a natural gift for understatement. He could find the humour in a situation, even in the darkest times.

Recounting his stories, Stoker never wanted to dwell too much on the atrocities he experienced. 'I've been sunk three times, once by the Japanese, once by the Yanks and once by the Aussies,' he would quip. This easy line hid the sad truth of what Stoker Munro and thousands of other Allied soldiers and sailors endured serving for their country in World War II. Yet Stoker's story is also unique. Aboard the *Perth* when it was torpedoed by the Japanese in 1942, Stoker survived drowning to be shipped to Changi; from Changi he went to work on the Thai–Burma Railway and survived that; from Thailand he was transported to Japan, where again the overcrowded rust-bucket vessel he was on attracted enemy fire – this time from American subs. That he lived to tell his tale makes him one of the lucky ones.

Like many men of the time, he kept his war to himself. Sometimes when we were talking he would just stop and sit there – I could only imagine what he was thinking, as he never showed any emotion. I have spoken to shipmates he served with after the war, as well as old friends who grew up with him in Byron Bay, and they all said the same thing: that he never discussed the war with them. Maybe he should have but that was his choice.

Stoker joined the RAN in June 1941 and did his training on HMAS *Cerberus* in Victoria, first in the Recruit School, then in the Marine Engineering School, where he learned the workings of engines and boilers. On completion he became officially known as 'Stoker' Munro, in a reference to the coal-fired boilers used on ships. In the navy, Stoker's nickname was 'Darby', after the famous jockey David 'Darby' Munro, but his family and friends called him Lloyd. To avoid confusion I have referred to him as I knew him, as Stoker Munro.

I feel privileged to have known him and have tried to faithfully relate Stoker's story in his own voice. I hope I have done him justice. To me he was an unexpected hero, a son of Australia and a true survivor.

HMAS *Perth*

HMAS Perth, *a light cruiser, was commissioned in the Royal Navy as HMS* Amphion *in June 1936. Australia purchased it to strengthen its naval forces and recommissioned it as HMAS* Perth *in Portsmouth, England, in June 1939. HMAS* Perth *reached Australia in March 1940, after early service in the Caribbean, the Pacific and in the Mediterranean, including evacuations of service personnel in Crete and Greece in April and May 1941.*

On 14 February 1942, under the command of Captain Hec Waller, HMAS Perth *sailed from Fremantle for the Dutch East Indies (now Indonesia), which was under threat from the advancing Japanese. The Battle of the Sunda Strait commenced in earnest on 28 February at 11.06pm when the Japanese invasion force assigned to western Java engaged and attacked the HMAS* Perth *and the USS* Houston. *The intensity of the battle was such that Captain Waller attempted a passage to safety through the approaching Japanese fleet. Shortly afterwards* Perth *was struck by four torpedoes and sank at 12.25am on 1 March 1942. Captain Waller died after a direct hit to the compass platform.*

The sinking of the Perth *cost the lives of 357 men. The nearby USS* Houston *was also torpedoed and sank in the early hours of 1 March*

1942. The survivors of both vessels became prisoners of war (POWs) of Japan, held captive in Java and Singapore, and most laboured on the infamous Thai–Burma Railway. Of the Perth *survivors, 106 died in captivity and 214 were finally repatriated to Australia.*

It is a fact that no member of the RAN ever received the Victoria Cross for an act of naval or military gallantry and valour.

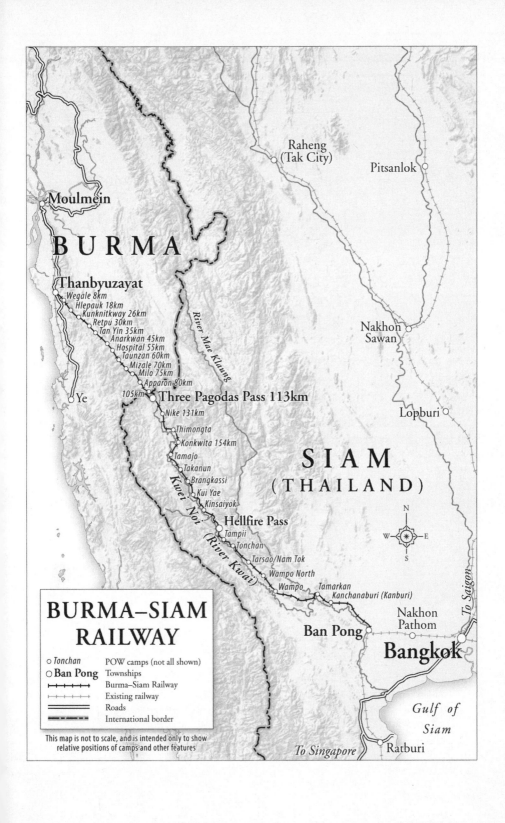

Raheng
(Tak City)

Pitsanlok

Moulmein

B U R M A

Thanbyuzayat
Wegale 8km
Hlepauk 18km
Kunknitkway 26km
Retpu 30km
Tan Yin 35km
Anarkwan 45km
Hospital 55km
Taunzan 60km
Mizale 70km
Milo 75km
Apparon 80km
105km   Three Pagodas Pass 113km

River Mae Klaung

Ye

Nike 131km
Thimongta
Konkwita 154km
Tamajo
Takanun
Brangkassi
Kui Yae
Kinsaiyok

Nakhon
Sawan

Lopburi

S I A M
(T H A I L A N D)

Kwei Noi

Hellfire Pass
Tampii
Tonchan
Tarsao/Nam Tok
Wampo North
Wampo   Tamarkan
Kanchanaburi (Kanburi)

(River Kwai)

N
W   E
S

Nakhon
Pathom

Ban Pong

To Saigon

Bangkok

BURMA–SIAM
RAILWAY

○ *Tonchan*   POW camps (not all shown)
◉ **Ban Pong**   Townships
├┼┼┤   Burma–Siam Railway
├┼┼┤   Existing railway
═══   Roads
▬▬▬   International border

This map is not to scale, and is intended only to show
relative positions of camps and other features

*Gulf of
Siam*

To Singapore   Ratburi

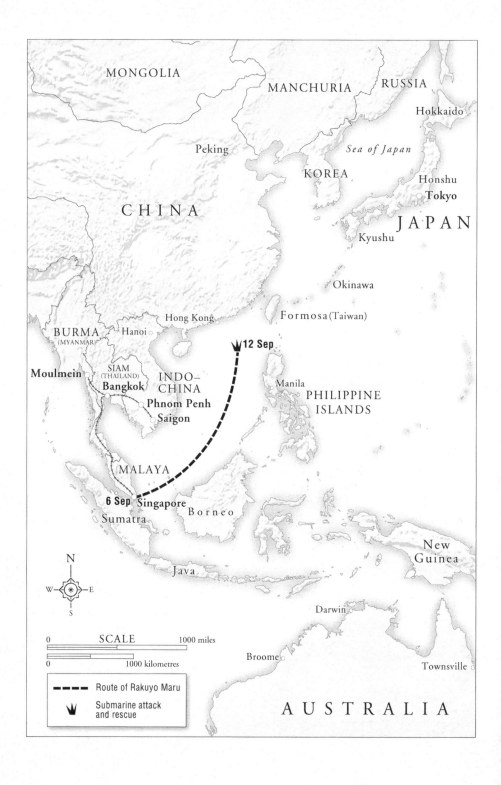

Chapter 1

On 13 February 1942, a hot Friday night, Stoker Lloyd 'Darby' Munro staggered onto a Fremantle dockside. He'd had a few beers, but the worst of it was that in naval terms he was, as of 1600 hours, officially 'adrift', absent without leave.

Vents hissed steam, men shouted orders, bulging cargo nets disappeared into holds and HMAS Perth *settled lower in the dark water. Stoker stared up at his ship readying itself for war, shifting the burden of his weight from one foot to the other as he took unsteady steps towards the gangway. He glanced at his wrist for his watch, the one his father had given him when he enlisted in the Royal Australian Navy. The watch wasn't there, his wrist was bare. Susan, a girl he'd met in a sailors' pub in Fremantle, had taken it – and his wallet – and all he could wonder was what his father would say when he told him he'd lost the watch, along with his virginity. All his shipmates had told him Susan was a troublemaker and now he knew why.*

A voice called from the darkness. 'You'd better hurry up, sailor, they're already singled up.'

Wharfies rushed about as I made my way onto the Fremantle dockside and then panic suddenly hit. I began to run towards the HMAS *Perth*, moored alongside, ready to sail, boilers charged and funnels belching steam. Cap in hand, I staggered straight up the gangway.

A dock worker stood with arm outstretched, reaching for the crane jib to remove the gangway. 'Just in time, son,' he said with a wink, moving aside to let me pass. I pulled on my cap and stepped on board, saluting the quarterdeck.

The master-at-arms roared above the noise. 'You're adrift, Stoker Munro! What's your excuse?'

'Caught me foot in the tram tracks, Master, and had to walk all the way to the junction before I could get it out.'

The master-at-arms glared at me; I can still see his clenched teeth. 'You're not funny, Munro. This ship is off to war and you'll find out that's not funny either. You're on Captain's Report, now get below.'

I made my way to the stokers' mess knowing I had not heard the last of it. The other stokers cheered as I climbed down the ladder.

One wag yelled, 'How did you go with Susan?'

I held up my arm, showing the white line on my suntanned wrist where my watch used to be.

'She got another one,' he crowed as they all laughed.

Knocka and Bomber, two blokes I went through Marine Engineering School with, helped me sling my hammock.

'You're in for it now, Stoker,' said Knocka.

I smiled like a silly fool and fell into the hammock, too drunk to care, too young to know how much trouble I'd brewed for myself. I told them to wake me up for my watch because I didn't want to be adrift again then collapsed. What seemed like only a few minutes later I felt rough hands on me and heard a voice that sounded far away. It was Knocka.

'Wake up, mate. The chief stoker wants to see you before you go on watch.'

The night before suddenly came back to me. I sat up and pulled on my overalls and new workboots, glancing down to admire the shiny naval-issue boots, my best. I knocked on the chief stoker's door and waited at attention outside. Leading Stoker George Grieve opened the door and told me the chief would see me. He warned me not to be a clever dick. Stepping inside, I found the chief at his desk writing in his log. I stood at attention but my head throbbed.

The chief looked up wearily. 'Are you going to be trouble for me, Munro?'

'No, Chief.'

'You've been aboard this ship for four months and you should know better than to tell the master-at-arms that cock-and-bull story about catching your foot in the tram tracks. If I can't depend on you I don't want you on my ship.'

'You can depend on me, Chief,' I blurted out.

'You're on Captain's Report and I hope he lashes you up good and proper. Now get on watch.'

I was about to walk out when he spoke again. 'Another thing, Munro. If you were with that troublemaker Susan in Fremantle, you present yourself to sick bay today and have an inspection, you follow me?'

I had no idea what he meant but agreed. 'Yes, Chief.'

After the *Perth* left port and sailed north, I heard a pipe over the speaker: 'Captain's Request men and defaulters fall in, Captain's flat.'

I squared myself off in my number-one uniform and presented myself to a junior engineering officer, Sub-lieutenant Stone, who was acting in my defence. There were six men appearing before the captain with their various requests for leave or promotion or whatever; I was the only defaulter.

Stone looked me up and down and asked, 'How do you plead, Munro?'

I told him I was guilty and got ready to face the music.

The master-at-arms called out, 'Stoker Munro, quick march.' We proceeded into the bridge. 'Halt! Off caps.'

I stood before senior officers arranged in a semicircle around the captain, Hec Waller. The master read out the charges, then Captain Waller turned to Sublieutenant Stone. 'How does he plead?'

'Guilty,' said Stone.

'You're lucky you made it back, Munro.' Captain Waller sounded cranky and spoke sternly. 'Why were you adrift?'

Adrift

'Sir, I had too much to drink, met a lady and took a punt we wouldn't sail on Friday the thirteenth. I heard that it's an old Royal Australian Navy tradition that we never sail on a black Friday.'

Captain Waller glared at me and said nothing for a bit. Then he got stuck in. 'Life is not a punt, Munro, it's about working together for the common good. On a ship, no link is too small, and if you think you're a man now, you'd better learn how to act like one. Master-at-Arms, this man is up for fourteen days' punishment and 28 days' stoppage of leave.'

'Aye-aye, sir,' I said, then the master-at-arms barked orders.

'Stoker Munro, on caps, about turn, quick march.'

We were sailing north, expecting to go as far as Singapore, when we received new orders. An unidentified ship had been reported and we were ordered to look for it. The buzz was that it was a German raider. Our Walrus reconnaissance plane was up searching but found nothing. Then we got new orders to escort some merchant ships back to Fremantle.

When we docked I asked Knocka to track down Susan the troublemaker and see if he could get my watch back. As the liberty men rushed off the ship and into the town of Fremantle I regretted my recent exploit; the bad news was Knocka never tracked down Susan, or my watch.

We left Fremantle on 17 February 1942 in company with HMAS *Adelaide* to escort three oil tankers bound for

Palembang, in southern Sumatra, to pick up oil. Halfway there news came through that Singapore had surrendered to the Japanese and that Java was now under attack. We were to escort the tankers back to Fremantle. Then new orders were received to leave them and proceed at full speed to Tanjung Priok, the main seaport in Batavia (now Jakarta). It was all very confusing. I had just turned eighteen and had been in the navy for seven months. When I joined I had expected to be fighting the Germans, but since the bombing of Pearl Harbor, barely two months earlier, Japan had quickly occupied the Philippines, Thailand, Vietnam and now Singapore. Japan was the new enemy and the feeling among the crew was that we were on a life-or-death mission to stop their advance to Australia.

From the captain down to the lowest sailor, we had no idea what awaited us in Tanjung Priok, when we arrived on 24 February. I had heard two old salts talking about the *Perth* having two chaplains on board at the same time, which was bad luck, an old navy superstition, and the harbour we sailed into, used for refuelling by Dutch, British, American and Australian troops, didn't look good. It was a ruin of bombed and sunken ships and heavily damaged wharves.

Captain Waller went ashore for a meeting. There was no one to meet. It turned out that the Dutch admiral in charge had moved his command post to near Bandung, up in the hills out of town. The officers returned dumbfounded and that's when the first Japanese planes appeared. They were just reconnaissance planes and they were gone in minutes. But more were soon to come.

In the meantime HMAS *Hobart* steamed in to refuel and join our battle fleet. It had to wait until we had finished refuelling, then our ship's boat was lowered and the chaplain, who was due to join the other ship, was put on board with mail for the *Hobart*. They were halfway there when a number of Jap bombers came over the horizon. Quickly the boat was called back and we were summoned to action stations. The Japs started their bombing runs and we fired back at them, only able to use our aft guns until they passed. All ships received orders to leave the harbour; we didn't have to be told twice. Quickly we cast off, still firing our guns. A couple of Dutch destroyers received hits from the Japs and one ran aground. The wharf area received a few hits too, with fuel bunkers exploding.

The air raid was over in fifteen minutes. It was my first time in action and it was not to be my last. I was scared.

The warships formed up out at sea. That night in the mess deck, one of the old salts told me that he'd seen the ship's cat trying to escape onto the wharf, and that was another bad sign; he said cats always knew something. Leading Stoker Grieve made a point of telling me to keep my money tin and life jacket close by at all times. Since I hadn't seen any other action, I couldn't imagine the sights or sounds of a real sea battle, but I didn't have long to wait.

The next day we steamed east towards Surabaya, to join the main Allied fleet under Admiral Doorman of the Dutch Navy, while HMAS *Hobart*, which had been unable to refuel because of the bombing, was ordered back to Fremantle. Surabaya turned out to be even more damaged than Tanjung Priok, but the combined American, British, Dutch, Australian fleet looked an impressive force to my eyes. In actual fact some of the ships were so old that if we had not been at war they would have been classified as obsolete.

On 26 February our ships left Surabaya to seek out the Jap invasion fleet reported to be coming from the east. It was a fruitless search, and after a day or so we returned to Surabaya. We had only a brief look at the port, because just as we entered we were ordered out and east again. Word had come through that the Japs had in fact been sighted. We met the fleet of transports, with soldiers ready for the invasion of Java, that night – the 27th. It was action stations – and no sleep – for over 24 hours.

In the fierce battle we lost a lot of ships, but miraculously the *Perth* suffered no damage. At one point, when the Japs withdrew temporarily, the Dutch admiral ordered some of our fleet to return to Surabaya for ammunition and to offload the injured. Not us, and when the Japs advanced again, it was slaughter for our smaller force. Still we remained undamaged. The only other ship to come out unscathed besides the *Perth* was the USS *Houston*, and together we headed back to Tanjung

Priok to refuel. In Tanjung Priok, we got an order to steam west into the Sunda Strait with USS *Houston* and that was where the real trouble began. We were headed straight for the Japanese invasion force that had been assigned to western Java. By this time it was the afternoon of 28 February and we were called to action stations again. The chief stoker was constantly on the blower, but he beckoned me over with a crook of his finger. You could hardly hear yourself think. He got in my ear and said, 'Go up and get some sangers and limers off the cooks.' I was starving and dehydrated from the heat, so I quickly climbed the ladder and opened the hatch door. One of the cooks stood there with a box of sandwiches. He looked really scared.

He said to me, 'We're in for it now, we've run into a Jap fleet. Take these.' He handed me the box. 'Come back up for your limers.'

I quickly went below and distributed sangers to the stokers, giving the chief stoker his first. He winked at me and smiled – it beat crying, I supposed. I went back up the ladder to where the cook stood with a ten-gallon fanny full of limers. 'Good luck, Stoker,' he said, handing me the aluminium bucket.

'Same to you, Chef.' I scooted back down with the salty, citrus-flavoured drink and walked around to each man, waiting while he dipped in his mug and scooped out as much as he wanted. When I came to the chief stoker he leaned over and said, 'You're doing a good job, Munro.' That made me feel better.

In the midst of contact with the Jap fleet we upped engine revolutions. I was on the sprayers, which controlled the amount of oil going into the boiler. We were on maximum power and had to hold on tight as the ship manoeuvred to port and starboard. Now I realised why they called the captain 'Hard Over' Hec.

Down in the boiler room we could feel the ship taking direct hits but had no idea of the damage being inflicted on us. The noise and heat were nearly unbearable. We had been at action stations for almost twelve hours before there was a lull in the action and I asked the chief stoker if I could go up to the heads to relieve myself.

'Be quick,' he said.

I scaled the ladder, which was very hot to the touch, and opened the boiler room door. Nothing in this world could have prepared me for what I saw. All the way from the sick bay, flat along the passageway, lay broken and bleeding men. The passageway was slick with so much blood it looked like a river. Some men were crying; others just lay there with their eyes wide open in shock. A few tried to help shipmates who were worse off than them, while others were clearly dead. There were nowhere near enough sick-berth attendants to look after them. I saw the cook who had brought the sangers lying there.

Up here I could clearly feel and hear our guns firing. I forgot all about going to the heads and went straight back to the boiler room. Our job was the most important one on the ship, which was to keep giving the skipper as much power as he needed. I had been on watch for eight hours. It seemed like forever. When you listened carefully you could hear our guns firing, but we were so busy tending the boilers we didn't notice them. It was only when our guns stopped firing that we wondered if the battle was over. We didn't know it then but our ship had run out of ammunition. Then we heard an unmistakable sound and felt the ship shudder – we had been hit by a torpedo. We all looked at one another then at the chief stoker, who appeared unflappable as he spoke on the blower to the bridge.

Suddenly we felt another torpedo hit for'ard, thanking God it was not amidships or we would all have been a goner. The ship slowly started to lose speed, even though we were giving her full power.

'The bow must have opened up,' one of the other stokers said when suddenly another torpedo hit us.

The chief stoker came and shouted in each stoker's ear. Finally he came to me and said, 'We're in trouble, son. Knock off the sprayers and shut the main stop. We're abandoning ship. Go up the escape hatch.'

If the boiler wasn't shut down properly it could explode and take a lot more lives with it. I quickly did what the chief told me and departed. We were among the last men to leave the boiler room by a ladder to the main deck.

I followed others to the rail and watched them jumping overboard into the night without a backwards glance. The

Perth was well alight and in the glare I saw heads bobbing all around us in the black sea. Fires forward and aft belched thick smoke, obscuring the bridge, but I looked up and saw Captain Waller on the compass platform. A moment later a salvo smashed into the platform, which disintegrated and took Captain Waller with it. I heard the cries of scared men yelling they couldn't swim, but they jumped in regardless. I pulled off my new boots, dropped them on the deck and, clutching my tobacco tin, jumped overboard, feet first. The water was pitch black and I had no idea how deep I went but I struggled back to the surface, bursting through the heavy bunker oil blanketing the water and swallowing a mouthful. The *Perth* was burning furiously and I knew I had to get away from her quickly. In the rush from the engine room I had left behind my kapok life jacket; it probably would have helped me float but hindered my swimming.

I made off about 100 yards where I heard voices calling for help in the dark, 'Over here, mate,' and others shouting, 'I love you, Mother!' Men yelled all around me but it was impossible to locate them because of the oil in my eyes; it was all I could do to keep my head above water. I swam as far as I could until I came up hard against a Carley float packed with dozens of men. A voice said, 'Just hold on, mate, there's no room on board.'

I grabbed a lifeline and trod water for an hour until I became so exhausted I almost let go, then someone reached down and hauled me aboard like a sack of spuds. They'd just pushed off a dead shipmate leaving room for me. 'Come on, mate, one off, one on.'

We were a good distance away from the sinking *Perth* when another torpedo slammed into it and we watched silently as our ship slid under. Suddenly we were alone at sea on a pitch-black night in an overcrowded Carley float. Someone said, 'Goodbye, gallant one.'

Fuel oil ran from my hair into my mouth and I could hardly see or breathe. I leant over the side and swilled seawater to flush the oil out of my mouth and throat, and even now, 60 years later, I still remember the taste of it. On the Carley float all I could make out were oil-blackened faces; everyone looked alike in the dark. No one spoke for a long while then I heard a familiar voice: 'Is that you, Stoker? It's me, Knocka.' He sobbed, 'Bomber didn't make it.' His war was over.

Every so often flashing guns on the USS *Houston* showed it was fighting back defiantly, but not long after it too was torpedoed, the mighty ship's prospects grim.

At daybreak we found ourselves surrounded by the floating dead, upturned rafts and *Perth* wreckage in the middle of an oil slick. I don't think hell has its equal. An officer with us, Sublieutenant Stone, had no idea what would happen next, but in the early light he asked each of us our name and if we were injured. On our raft were men who had suffered horrible burns and open wounds, but we could do very little to help any of them. When the morning mist rose we saw the Sumatran coast in the distance. Those of us fit enough tried paddling the raft by hand, but we made no headway against the current and watched the coast disappear.

A ship appeared on the horizon that we thought could be either HMAS *Yarra*, which we knew was in the vicinity, or a Japanese destroyer looking for survivors. We hoped it was *Yarra* and looked for the white ensign on the stern, but instead saw the Rising Sun of Nippon fluttering in the breeze. We feared the Japs turning their guns on us and some of the men began sobbing. I heard a few prayers when the destroyer closed in, with no idea what the Japanese sailors lining the rails would do next. They stood off about 50 yards and their engines slowed and stopped. A voice called out in English that those of us who were able to should abandon the float and climb the nets lowered over the side. A boat was sent out to pick up the wounded and non-swimmers and haul them aboard. The rest of us swam to the ship in a calm sea and climbed the nets. After they pushed our float away I hoped someone else might use it because there had to have been many more survivors than just our little group.

Once aboard, Knocka gave me a hug. 'We made it, mate.'

'So far, Knocka, but this is just beginning.'

We assembled on the quarterdeck, most of us naked and completely coated in congealed oil. The Japanese sailors gave us buckets of kerosene and rags to clean it off, and some thin 'short-time' towels the size of dishcloths that we used like nappies, for dignity's sake. Later they gave us mugs of hot black tea while a Japanese sailor walked among us and issued cigarettes then lit them for us. I drank my tea and puffed on my fag and wondered what they were saving us for.

The Japanese captain, dressed in an immaculately pressed white uniform, appeared and surveyed us. Sublieutenant Stone stepped forward in his nappy, introduced himself as our group's senior officer and saluted the Japanese officer, who returned his salute. 'Sir, I insist we be treated under the terms of the Geneva Convention.'

The officer replied in perfect English. 'The Imperial Japanese Navy respects you as warriors. We will treat you as such but the Imperial Japanese Government is not a signatory to the Geneva Convention.' He walked among us, looked at our wounded and assigned Japanese medics to tend to burns and other injuries. 'Tomorrow we transfer you to the Imperial Japanese Army. You will learn they are not as humane as we are.'

He looked dead serious when he said that, even sad. He barked out an order and two cooks approached carrying pans of boiled rice. They scooped it into our mugs and we ate with our fingers. The captain waved his arm towards the horizon and told Sublieutenant Stone there were likely more survivors to rescue. Stone saluted and thanked him.

The captain set watches on all points searching for survivors. We cruised slowly through the floating wreckage of the remains of the *Perth* and *Houston* and saw many dead sailors face down and fully clothed, now in the grip of a current setting strongly for the Indian Ocean. The ship changed course often and when it slowed we tried to stand to have a look, but the guards raised their weapons with fixed bayonets. The message was clear: stay down and away from the rails. We felt the ship turn hard. Japanese sailors rushed to port and pointed to a Carley float with men aboard, American sailors from the *Houston*, mostly nude and covered in oil.

Once they'd been brought aboard, Knocka and I helped one bloke peel off his dungarees. He had no wounds but he was pretty buggered and could hardly stand. We got him undressed and when I tried to toss his shirt overboard he gripped my hand and whispered that there was something in the front pocket, his wallet. I felt for it and he grabbed it from me, thanking me quietly. Japanese sailors brought out kerosene and rags, the towels and then tea and cigarettes for the new prisoners.

We introduced ourselves to the new bloke. 'I'm Stoker Lloyd Munro from the *Perth* and this is my mate Stoker Knocka White.'

'Slim, from the USS *Houston*.'

'We know that, you silly bugger,' Knocka said.

Slim was much older than either of us, a career sailor, and I knew right away we'd get on.

He looked at our nappies and laughed. 'We call these G-strings where I come from.' Knocka and I had never heard that before, and soon everyone was calling them G-strings. Slim didn't say much, puffing on his cigarette and staring out to sea. 'That mess was all the Dutch admiral's fault, you know,' he muttered. 'He should never have split up his fleet because that cost two fine ships, all avoidable.'

Knocka and I were just young stokers down the hole; we knew nothing of what had really happened in the battle we'd just survived. Slim had been a senior radio operator on the *Houston* and privy to the chatter back and forth. 'It will all come out one day,' was all he said. I used to wonder what he meant, and only after the war learned the details of how that Dutch admiral made us vulnerable by dividing the fleet and underestimating the enemy: two fatal errors.

The tropical sun heated the steel deck until it burned our feet. Under captain's orders sailors played out a stream of cold sea water from a fire hose to cool the deck while they continued to pick up survivors until we numbered roughly 200. Their respectful treatment of us surprised everyone. The destroyer zigzagged all day but by late afternoon we stopped finding any more signs of life or manned floats, and around dusk the engine upped revolutions and we steamed away at top speed. The breeze made for a pleasant night on deck, almost idyllic, but on waking the next morning I remembered the reality: we were prisoners of war.

I asked Slim what the captain of the Japanese destroyer meant when he said the army might not treat us well. He told us that the Imperial Japanese Army followed a code of behaviour from the ancient samurai warriors called *bushido*: they'd rather commit suicide than surrender and had no respect for prisoners. Not like the navy. Slim knew a lot more about the world than two young sailors from Australia but he never said more than he had to.

He wondered aloud where we'd end up and Knocka reckoned Singapore.

'Singapore? No, too far away. Probably Batavia, it's closer. If we want to get through whatever happens next, we better stick together.'

I remember saying, 'Bloody oath, I'm too young to die.'

'He's the baby of the ship,' said Knocka.

'How old, Stoker?' Slim asked.

'Eighteen years and one month.'

Slim looked me up and down; I was only eighteen but just a shade under six feet four. He whistled through his perfect teeth. I can still see those teeth, white as pearls and plenty of them.

In the afternoon we sailed into Banten Bay, a small fishing port near Tanjung Priok, which was filled with wrecked Japanese vessels from the invasion force. I remember thinking that our bombers were doing a good job. We tied up alongside the *Somedong Maru*, a rusting transport ship manned by armed Japanese soldiers waiting to lead us aboard. As we crossed from the destroyer to the *Somedong Maru*, sailors collected our mugs and bowed respectfully to each man. Just minutes later, aboard the hulk, Japanese soldiers shouted at everyone, including the injured, and prodded the slow blokes with their rifles. None of us understood any Japanese so our reply to all taunts was always silence, although we soon began to understand new words: *tenko,* headcount, and *speedo,* quickly. Some soldiers stared at us as if we were the first westerners they'd ever seen. We were all barefoot on the hot deck so had to hop from foot to foot, and the guards thought that was bloody hilarious. The bastards laughed so hard they bent over double, holding their stomachs.

Suddenly the captain of the destroyer appeared on his bridge and shouted. The soldiers stopped laughing quick smart and rolled out hoses to spray the deck with cool seawater. Not long after, as the destroyer slowly left port, we saw the captain waving but none of us waved back. Looking back I believe we should have acknowledged his wave; he'd saved our lives and treated us decently.

The army blokes, on the other hand, were not nearly as chivalrous and we knew we were in for it. They herded us down a ladder backwards into the fetid hold where it was hot, damp and crowded. Slim, Knocka and I found space on the shaded side and sat on bare steel plate. Above us there was only a small hatch, and with no cross breeze or ventilation it was stifling. This space was to be used as a holding cell till they could decide what to do with us. We were only allowed on deck to use the *benjo*, a toilet jerry-built of two wooden planks hanging over the side and lashed to the rail. Blokes constantly climbed the ladder to relieve themselves and get a breath of fresh air. Our medic tried to help the wounded and shouted up through the hatch that he had many burned men needing bandages and medical supplies. Three guards peered down at the medic and he asked again. The guards said nothing; they disappeared and didn't come back, and two of our men died that night.

'That's the way the army does it,' said Slim. 'No respect for prisoners.'

Fresh water came down in a bucket with one cup and later that evening they lowered two buckets of boiled rice to feed all 200 of us. Since we had no utensils we used tobacco tins or our hands. I recall that gluey rice clearly; I never got used to it, but it filled a hole.

In the morning we were ordered onto the wharf for *tenko* – the headcount. With the language barrier, they kept getting the count wrong till we showed them our two dead. They had a good laugh. We buried the dead and the soldiers loaded us onto five overcrowded trucks, including the wounded and burned. We did what we could to comfort them but we were so crowded in that the burned men suffered horribly, and the trip to god-knew-where over rough roads must have been almost unbearable for them.

Chapter 2

We left Banten Bay and drove over rutted roads through shady forests and little villages. After about an hour we saw a road sign for Serang, 80 kilometres, a place no one knew anything about. We slowed down going through villages, and some Javanese jeered while others waved or threw bananas into the trucks. We stopped after crossing a stream and the guards allowed us off to take care of our needs. A couple of blokes climbed a nearby mango tree and tossed down as many as they could grab and, to curry favour, we gave some to the guards. When men bent to drink at the stream the senior medic rushed over and told them not to; he reckoned we had to boil the water first. But their thirst meant that few listened, and dysentery soon ran rife throughout the troops. Slim said he'd take the word of the medic. Somehow Slim had an air of authority and I decided to do what he did.

The next *tenko* turned out to be another comedy. The guards counted three times and looked confused, but at last the sergeant gave the order to leave. We arrived at Serang, a little village, late in the afternoon and parked outside an old prison. The sergeant guarding the convoy went inside and we waited for half an hour until he came out then unloaded about twenty prisoners including Knocka. I felt bad being separated from my little mate. We had been together since Recruit School. The sergeant jumped back in the lead truck and we started off again. One wag yelled, 'No more room at the inn.'

We drove for a few minutes and stopped at an old cinema. The guards shouted, '*Speedo!*' and we jumped down, lining up again for *tenko*. They counted three times and concluded two were missing. The sergeant disappeared and a minute later came out followed by his superior, the furious camp commandant, who took a long look at us and then suddenly slapped the sergeant's face. It was no longer a comedy for him. After a final headcount they marched us into the cinema, which was crowded with about 300 POWs from the *Perth* and *Houston*. Men from both saw shipmates they presumed had drowned. Cries of 'Good on you' echoed throughout the cinema and men embraced, glad to be alive. Later we heard that the Japanese had it right, their count was off by two; a couple of Yanks had taken off into the jungle at the rest stop and we never heard what happened to them.

Most of the POWs here were also dressed in G-strings and still covered in oil, and I recognised only one bloke at first, Leading Stoker Grieve. We shook hands, happy we'd made it, and he told me to call him George as we traded stories. His float had washed up on a Sumatran beach where some locals gave him food and water. He hoped they might hide him, but they had been warned by the Japanese Land Army and turned him over. It happened to most survivors. I introduced him to Slim and they shook hands like long-lost brothers. I told George that Slim was from Texas and was a survivor from the *Houston*. Slim said, 'Pleased to meet you, bloke.' George had a laugh.

George had been here for two days and gave us the drum on the drill at the cinema. Boiled rice was all we got and we slept on bare concrete floors while mossies sucked our blood. He pointed to the upper lounge where guards trained three machine guns down on us all, by now nearly 500 men with us new arrivals. Latrines out the back were wooden planks straddling a mud pit and we had nowhere to wash; it wasn't pretty. The Jap navy hadn't been able to kill us but it looked like disease might.

George talked about work parties that went outside, where there were opportunities for trade if you had money, but you needed to bribe the guards and none of us had clothes (which the Jap guards might have been interested in for their insignia) let alone money of any sort, except for Slim who still had his wallet bulging with cash. Slim reckoned getting out for a breath of fresh air might do the trick. He wanted to go out to meet the POWs from the crowded old jail where Knoka had gone, who would be a source of information. George told him to rise early and be near the cinema doors and 'have a chat' with the guard.

Our officers couldn't do anything for us because the Japs only respected rank, and since we looked the same with no insignias, it was a lost battle. A few officers tried talking to the sergeant of the guard about conditions but it turned into a shouting match, and an uneven one at that. No one understood the other and two guards knocked a few of our officers about until one of the Yank officers calmed them down. We were on a sticky wicket there for a bit. On that first day five blokes died from their burns and injuries. We didn't have much to look forward to except our daily rice, even though we had to eat it with our fingers.

On our first night in the cinema we were again stretched out like sardines in a can, with the concrete floor as a bed and swarms of mosquitoes as a blanket. I still slept.

The banging of the cinema doors opening woke me. I looked around for Slim and saw him up near the doors talking with a Jap guard. Other men who wanted to go out on the work parties gathered around. They got their ration first off the cooks then out they went.

Each morning the Japs conducted their *tenko* which took them forever; it was like a circus. Later one of our officers came up to George and me and six other men and announced we were required for a work party. We would have done anything to get out in the fresh air. We followed him to the doors where two Jap guards were waiting and marched out, our officer in the lead and guards following. They soon stopped us and the smell revealed where we were going: the latrine pit. We looked down at the waste of 500 men, a moving mass of maggots. One of our men vomited his morning ration back up. Another bloke reached down for the undigested rice.

'Can't waste it, it's still warm,' he said as he shoved it down his throat.

'He won't last long,' George whispered to me.

Right then. We had to cover this. There were a couple of old shovels which two blokes grabbed. The rest of us had to improvise, using pieces of wood to scrape dirt from the surrounding area. After about three hours of digging and scraping we managed to cover the pit with a layer of soil. It had been hot work. We retreated to a shady area and watched our officer smoking and laughing with the guards.

I looked up and said, 'I wondered what he meant when he said we had a job to do.'

George replied, 'How long have you been in the navy?'

'I know, don't do as I do, do as I say.'

Our officer, noticing us, walked down to inspect our work. 'Good job, men,' he said. 'Now listen, I've managed to get a reward out of the guards for you, a cigarette each, so when they come to inspect your work and give you your cigarette, just bow your head and thank them.'

'Like bloody hell we will,' we all said together.

Our answer perplexed him; it was probably the first time he had been spoken to like that by ratings. He just stood there thinking for a bit, then he said, 'Well, just smile and thank them.'

He walked back and brought the guards down to see our work. Slowly they walked towards us with noses sniffing the air. Our job was good for everyone – fewer flies. True to the officer's word we were handed a cigarette each with great ceremony by the guards. The bloke who ate the spew puffed on his straight away. The rest of us kept ours to share inside the cinema with other mates.

We marched back to the cinema and, while waiting for the doors to be opened, were able to look around at the town. There wasn't much: a few run-down stores, a handful of people and a couple of dogs playing and fighting with one another. The Jap guard picked up stones and tossed them at the dogs, which only infuriated them and made them snarl at the guards. One of the dogs made a move in their direction and a guard unslung his rifle and shot it. At the sound of the shot, guards ran from everywhere. When they saw what had happened they all had a good laugh before going back to their posts. The Japs sure had a perverse sense of humour. Little did we know that in six months' time we would have gratefully eaten that dead dog.

There was a solitary street vendor selling iceblocks. Our officer negotiated with the guards to buy some with what money we had and they agreed, but the vendor wouldn't be in it. He kept shouting even after the cinema doors shut behind us and we went through yet another *tenko*. Later we heard that an earlier work detail had paid the street vendor with Australian pennies, not the Dutch guilders he'd expected. The vendor had been so busy the men had got away with it but we learned if we wanted to buy anything we had to use threepenny bits or anything silver; that did the trick.

One afternoon Slim returned with a work party wearing a shirt and trousers, his G-string tied like a turban around his head. After *tenko* he told us he'd bought the clothes from a Dutch-Indonesian who liked Yankee dollars. He pulled out a pawpaw, a packet of Dutch cigarettes and three spoons from his pockets and handed them over; it saved us from eating with our fingers. He took off the turban and looked at us seriously. 'I know I can trust you two, but this is a matter of life and death.'

He unwound the turban and showed us his secret: a radio. Slim was thrilled with it, but getting caught with a radio meant instant execution, decapitation with a samurai sword; he'd taken a huge risk.

We heard shouting and the doors opened and two Japanese guards leading the camp commandant forced a passage through the crowded cinema. The commandant swaggered in carrying a samurai sword as long as he was tall. He shouted in English for our senior officers to come forward. Eight officers from the *Perth* and *Houston* made their way through the crowd. One tried to talk to the commandant but a guard shoved his bayonet into the officer's chest and drew blood. Another officer shouted at the soldier to leave his officer alone and then the guards upstairs swung the machine guns in an arc around the cinema. For a minute there we had a standoff. It wouldn't have taken much to wipe us all out.

The commandant started speaking and the cinema quietened down. 'You men bring dishonour to your country. Japanese soldiers never surrender; we prefer to die than accept imprisonment.' He stared at the sea of faces before him, then narrowed his eyes and took a breath. 'Imperial Japanese Army will soon be in Australia. We already bomb Darwin and Broome, very soon, Brisbane and Perth.'

We stood silently, he had our full attention. There was no way of knowing if he was telling the truth or not, but we exchanged looks, disbelieving although unsure. Some with family left behind cried at the thought.

'You cannot escape, there is nowhere to go. If just one man tries to escape,' he pulled out his samurai sword two-handed, raised it above his head and swung it downwards and simulated a decapitation, 'then you will *all* die.'

The machine gunners above him screamed in unison, *'Banzai! Banzai! Banzai!'*

Our senior officer marched forward, halted and saluted. 'Sir, many of my men are burned, malnourished and ill. They must have better food, clean water, washing facilities and regular exercise.'

The commandant stared at the officer. For his answer he spun on his heels and stormed out, surrounded by guards. The moment the doors closed behind him the cinema buzzed.

'Do you think the Japs bombed Australia?' I asked.

Slim reckoned they could; it wasn't that far to Darwin and Broome. George was shaken; he had a wife in Sydney and family in Brisbane. No one knew any better, so anything seemed possible. The Japanese had moved quickly.

One senior officer shouted above the noise. 'Listen, men, back home there are still a lot of men in uniform, it won't be easy for the Japs. Have faith, we can't believe everything they say. They told us we were going to a holiday camp.' He spread his arms out. 'Does this look like a holiday camp?'

Some shouted, 'No!'

'We have to stick together and look after one another as Aussies do. Now the padre wants to say a few words.'

I hardly recognised the chaplain in his G-string. He spoke softly and told us he would like us to dedicate a prayer to those at home wondering if we were alive or dead and that they be protected from invasion. He led us, believers and non-believers, through the Lord's Prayer, and at the end there were plenty of tears shed. Then he moved among us to give comfort.

Slim rewrapped his radio in the G-string and made his way to the back of the cinema, where the officers were. He returned wearing only his G-string in its original position. Grabbing the pawpaw, Slim cut it in three with his spoon and shared it with us. I asked about the missing shirt and trousers and he said he gave them to our chaplain, who needed the dignity more than he did. Our pawpaw went down well with the boiled rice and nothing more was said about the radio.

Next morning, Slim was at the front doors again, waiting to join a work party while the Japs did the morning *tenko* once and then again; they never seemed to get it right the first time. The sergeant went into a rage and stormed out, returning with a very unhappy-looking commandant. He screamed for attention and they counted again: the headcount wasn't wrong, there'd been an escape.

'I told you, anybody escapes and we not find, you all die, all die!' The commandant calmed down. 'If here, better come now, we find, no escape.'

Our silence infuriated him. None of us knew about an escape and we said nothing. He marched out behind his guard and as the doors shut behind him a few men laughed quietly. The officer in charge of the latrine party said we didn't want to antagonise the commandant but he laughed too. Then we heard that the escapee was Wireman Fred Lasslett from HMAS *Perth*. Someone immediately started a book on Lasslett's chances, the longest odds given on him staying away for more than a day.

That night the doors banged open and a bloodied and beaten Lasslett was dragged in by Jap guards and paraded before the men, then they dragged him back outside. The sergeant made

45

a chopping motion with his hand to let us know what his fate would be. He stood for a bit then banged the door shut behind him. I knew Lasslett; I'd agree he was a bit of a chancer but a good man for all that, and he didn't deserve to die for 'having a go'. To say we were stunned is an understatement, and for the next half hour everyone shut up and retreated into private thoughts of the impending horror.

Next morning, while Slim went on his work party wearing his G-string, George and I went back to working at the latrine. While we worked we asked our officer what would happen to Lasslett.

'You heard what the Japs said, he put us all in danger. They'll top the bastard.'

'But, sir, isn't our job to try to escape?'

'Yes, within reason, but not if you put us all at risk. Anyway, where's he going? You'd have to be well prepared and depend on locals, and they believe the Japs are here for their benefit. The Japs really only want their oil fields, the locals will learn. Enough chat – all hands to, let's get this job done.'

Once we put our backs into it he wandered over to talk with the guards, away from the smell. While scraping up the dirt we sweated in the heat and attracted clouds of mossies looking for blood. We finished the job and found shade near the galley, basically a tarpaulin under which cooks stoked a fire heating a 44-gallon drum of water. I was thirsty and cupped my hands to take a drink from it when a petty officer cook from the *Perth* told me the water hadn't been boiled yet, passing me a mug of water instead. The drum was filled with jars and empty tins, to be used as dixies for meals once sterilised. That night, medics advised us not to share mugs or dixies to prevent spreading disease if we wanted to survive.

With no books we became bored in short order and blokes became inventive, drawing draught boards on the floor with a burned stick and using nut husks and leaves as men, while an artist sketched on a wall. The rest of us tried to rest and preserve our energy, ignoring the ever-circulating rumours.

Slim came back from a work party wearing a new shirt and trousers, his G-string once again a turban. He unravelled his turban and showed us the spare valves he'd bought from a local, saying we shouldn't worry about the Japs finding the radio, it wouldn't be there long. I knew enough to not ask what he meant. The radio would be our window into how the war was going. Before lights out Slim disappeared into the officers' area with the valves. I wondered if we'd ever get to hear the radio but decided it was too dangerous; we'd just take the news as it came on the grapevine.

Slim produced a little something almost every time he went out. His best score was a single duck breast that had been cooked in soya sauce, sliced thinly and wrapped in a banana leaf before being smuggled into the cinema in his turban. When Slim said it was the best he could get, we almost cheered. For our little group that duck was a feast, and eating duck meat and rice out of a sterilised jar was almost like being back in civilisation.

A senior officer from HMAS *Perth* came to speak to me about the death of Captain Waller so he could document it. He asked to hear my version of events. I told him I looked up and saw the captain on the port bridge span, watching his men abandoning ship, when a salvo dropped right on top of him and I never saw him again. I said there were fires burning fore and aft and the night was like daytime. He thanked me and left.

'I saw my captain dead too,' Slim said. 'Captain Rooks, best skipper I ever served with.'

'Well, Captain Waller was my *only* skipper. "Hard Over" Hec, we called him.'

Next morning the cinema doors opened and we heard a big commotion, shouting and laughing. The escapee, Wireman Lasslett, walked into the cinema wearing a bandana with Japanese characters on it and dressed in a new shirt and shorts. He even had a tool bag hanging off his hip. Later on we heard his story. He got about two miles away and hid in the jungle until villagers found him and gave him up to the Japs, who had a reward out for any Allied servicemen. He was paraded before the commandant and at that exact moment the lights failed, a camp-wide blackout, every light in the place. Lucky for Lasslett he was a qualified electrician and said he could fix the lights, and did so in minutes. The commandant commuted his sentence and made him the camp electrician. They wrote 'Camp Electrician' on his bandana, and from then on he was known as 'Lucky' Lasslett.

In the stifling heat of the cinema he worked for a few hours and got the fans working, which did wonders for our morale. Even the commandant came to watch the fans moving. We gave Lucky a huge cheer and the commandant thought we were cheering him, which made him happy. After that the guards were less severe with us and green vegetables sometimes appeared in our daily rations. Slim brought back cigarettes and the occasional tin of pickled herrings to add a bit of variety to our rice diet, improving our small group's spirits, but George and I still had to tend to the latrines and conditions were at best grim. Men came down with dysentery and malaria, and at night the delirious called for their mothers. It became a living nightmare for everyone, and the burial parties were kept busy because we lost at least one man a night.

The Japs supplied us with a form of soap and allowed us out in bathing parties to a stream behind the cinema. Some men covered in oil scrubbed themselves so hard they removed layers of skin and looked as if they'd been burned with a blowtorch. We learned later that the stream was used by the locals as a garbage and sewer disposal, and infection spread immediately.

After six weeks in the cinema, a small Japanese officer attended by a squad of armed soldiers addressed us in perfect English. He said how sorry he was to have kept us under such conditions but he had good news. 'Tomorrow you will all be sent to a new camp where there will be a proper kitchen with plenty of food. I know you Australians like meat and sports and you will find sports fields there to play on, to make you fit so you can work for the Emperor.'

He bowed, saluted us and left. We didn't know what to make of the Japanese. George said it sounded like another holiday camp, but anything had to be better than this awful cinema.

True to their word, next morning, 13 April 1942, we heard trucks drawing up outside. A great sense of excitement swept the cinema and we were ready to move in minutes – it's not as if we had much to take with us, just our dixies and what little stuff we kept. As we left the cinema we were counted again and loaded onto too few trucks. Confusion reigned until they sent a large group, including us, back into the cinema. Mid-morning more trucks arrived and the remaining POWs climbed into a half-full truck. The first face I saw was Knocka White, who had been in the old jail. We shook hands.

'Christ, Stoker, you're skin and bones.'

'Don't you talk, Knocka, you look like shit.'

'Well, that's all I have been doing for the last two weeks. The doc says I have dysentery. Can I sit on the edge? I have no control over my bowels.'

We hadn't seen each other for six weeks and each other's physical condition alarmed us both, but six weeks turned out to be a short time in our journey.

'Lucky' Lasslett becomes camp electrician at Serang Cinema

The Japs gave each of us a packet of cigarettes and a portion of bread for the journey. We drove past the cemetery and the sight of the many crude crosses on the graves of our shipmates made me realise how lucky I was. We drove through forests and villages; it was a beautiful part of the world. Some locals threw us fruit and the Jap guards and drivers looked the other way. When the trucks stopped for toilet breaks the guards kept a close eye on us; no chance to escape. We passed through bigger villages and glimpsed the ocean every so often as we went up hills and down to the flat lands. Eventually we drove into a bigger town and it seemed we were in the capital, Batavia.

We pulled up outside a large camp and saw men wearing slouch hats. The guards called, '*Speedo, speedo*,' as we climbed down from the trucks, and the laggards got a poke in the ribs with rifle butts.

Slim spoke to a soldier and was clubbed in the back by a Japanese guard.

'No speak!' the guard shouted.

Soldiers of the Australian 7th Division swarmed around the fence to see the new arrivals and they stared at us; six weeks in the cinema on a poor diet had turned us into skin and bone. They stood open-jawed at the sight of us; some blokes cried. They hadn't known about the sinking of the *Perth* and had been vainly waiting for it to evacuate them. The guards held a final *tenko* before we entered the camp.

Our officers lined up and saluted a uniformed Australian Army officer and he returned their salute as if they were on a parade ground. We were the second batch from the cinema so he was already aware of our condition. The officer told us we'd 'be right' from now on.

'This is the Bicycle Camp, because it once housed a Dutch Bicycle Regiment barracks. Here we have decent food and plenty of room.' We cheered. 'We have a hospital,' more cheers, 'and hot showers,' and that brought the loudest cheer of all.

Some wag called out, 'No women, sir?' Even the officers laughed.

Although we observed military protocol in the Bicycle Camp and respected rank, we had only one thing in mind: keeping body and soul together. Our sick were stretchered away to the hospital; the rest of us had to fill in forms with our name, rank and official number.

Aussie soldiers were gathered around us when a voice I knew called out. 'Lloyd? It's Jimmy from the *Wollongbar*.'

I recognised the familiar voice immediately. 'I know who you are, you silly bastard.' Tears welled up.

I'd have known him from thirty yards. He sailed out of Byron Bay on the coaster *Wollongbar* and was partly responsible for my interest in going to sea. We shot the breeze for a minute or two and then he stepped back and took a long look at me, wanting to know what had happened to the fit young man he knew in Byron Bay.

I wasn't sure where to begin. 'Still standing,' I eventually said, and we had a laugh.

We went to hospital for check-ups, and Knocka was promptly admitted to the infectious diseases ward. I told him he would be alright. I wasn't confident: his eyes were sunken and he could hardly walk. The rest of us took doses of quinine for malaria and were issued clean shorts, shirts, a toothbrush and a towel and taken to the showers, our first in six weeks. A few razors appeared and after a shave we all looked a lot younger. That shower was better than any sex I might have had with that 'troublemaker' in Fremantle, and it was good to smell a clean towel. I saw the camp barber, and the Aussie soldiers who were captured with full kit and plenty of extras gave us their spare clothes. I no longer had to hide my tobacco tin in the G-string, just slid it into my shorts' pocket. Jimmy looked us over and said we were 'as good as new', then led us to the mess tent where the cooks had a meal ready.

After the chaplain led us in a prayer of thanksgiving, we sat and a plate was put in front of me, meat and three veg. I'd dreamed about it for six weeks and got stuck in. Pretty soon you could have heard a pin drop as we ate our first decent meal in ages, afterwards rubbing our guts and burping from the lemonade. We might have sung a few songs too. Then we each got a mug of hot tea and a one-pound block of Cadbury's chocolate. With 300 men belching at the same time, sounding like a bad symphony, dinner turned into a laughing party.

Later we sat outside in the shade smoking cigarettes with our new army chums. Jimmy wanted to know about the loss of HMAS *Perth*. I told him how we crowded on a Carley float hoping that the approaching ship was the *Yarra* and not Japanese.

'So you haven't heard that the Japs bombed the *Yarra*? She's gone.'

'How do you know?'

'We hear news from home on a couple of radios.'

He whispered that the Japs had bombed Darwin and Broome, and confirmation of that rumour hit us for six. He'd heard nothing about an invasion of Australia, but he knew about the fall of Singapore and that over 100,000 men had been taken prisoner with very few escapees. He'd heard rumours along the way that some senior AIF officers were tipped the nod and had flown back home on transports just hours before the fall.

Jimmy's time at sea on the *Wollongbar* meant he was suited to join the RAN, but when he enlisted he heard Australia needed soldiers more, so that was his destiny. He'd served in Egypt and North Africa, where Australia lost many fighting the Italians and Rommel's elite Afrika Korps. When the Japs entered the war the prime minister, John Curtin, ordered Australian troops home in convoys, and Jimmy was one of 600 aboard the British troopship *Orcades* on its way back to Australia when they were diverted to Batavia. The soldiers were offloaded to help the Dutch resist the encroaching Japanese forces. The *Orcades* sailed off without them and those remaining were told that the *Perth* would pick them up, but we were sunk in the Sunda Strait and they waited in vain. When the Japs invaded, the Dutch surrendered with not one shot discharged in defence, and suddenly Jimmy was another POW.

We were full and tired and followed Jimmy to large barracks filled with cots and men sleeping under mosquito nets and blankets. I found an empty cot and sank into it for my first decent sleep in comfort in months.

Chapter 3

After three weeks my weight shot up a stone due to regular meals, and the health of most of the sick men improved, except for my mate Stoker Knocka White, who'd been holed up in sick bay almost since we arrived at Bicycle Camp. Sublieutenant Stone came to see me with the sad news: my shipmate Knocka had died of dehydration as a result of dysentery. He said that I could be in the burial party if I wanted and to be at the hospital at colours in the morning – 8am (in the RAN), when the flag is raised. Knocka had left me his watch and tobacco tin. I liked Knocka White's easy smile and laugh and his death brought me great sadness, but no tears. Death was so frequent by now I only had one emotion left and that was surviving.

At 0800h George, me and two others from *Perth* mustered at the hospital to carry Knocka's coffin to the graveyard, followed by Chaplain Mathieson from HMAS *Perth*. I'll always remember the mounds of newly dug graves marked with wooden crosses; there would be many more to come. In Knocka's tobacco tin I found a few quids worth of change and a set of three Crown and Anchor dice. George reckoned they might come in handy one day and I was so green around the gills that I wondered how.

A few days later we heard a loud sound in the distance, a chorus of men singing 'The Yellow Rose of Texas'. Some ten minutes later 600 American soldiers from the 131st Field Regiment, in full uniform, wheeled into the Bicycle Camp. Our men rushed to the wire and watched them march in. Slim said they weren't Yanks but Texans, like him, but we didn't know any different and called them Yanks anyway. Our officers greeted the new arrivals and Slim spoke with them, learning that they were in good condition and had brought two truckloads of supplies, later shared with the Aussie pool. We were walking around half-naked and were especially interested in boots and whatever else they had in their kitbags.

HMAS *Perth* had escorted the 131st Field Regiment convoy from Fiji to Australia in 1941, before I served on her, so the 131st felt a special bond with our ship. They were ordered to Batavia from Australia in 1942 with a specific goal to protect the Shell oil refineries, but when the Dutch left them high and dry the Japanese captured them holus-bolus.

Slim produced a bottle of bourbon whisky, opened it and we polished off half in memory of Knocka. I noticed that Slim had a new pair of boots, GI issue, and said I'd like a pair, size 12. He said, with a wink, to give him time. He was always quick on his feet, old Slim, and rarely came back from any detail without something to be smoked, eaten or drunk. I asked him what it was like growing up in Texas, which seemed so far away, almost mythical; our only idea of it was from western movies seen at the pictures. I had visions of cattle ranches and open spaces but he set me right. His parents were both born and bred in the city of Houston and he was raised on the Gulf of Mexico. His father worked as a rigger in oilfields all over Texas. There were five kids in the family and not much money, so in the mid-thirties, with his parents' blessing, he joined the navy and was posted to the USS *Houston*. The whole neighbourhood knew all about the *Houston*, ever since President Roosevelt had spent a couple of weeks aboard. Slim had been in the navy for seven years, starting in the radio room and rising through the ranks to senior operator. In that position he soon learned his way around, including how things really worked in the chain of command.

When Slim mentioned that the Texans had money, George suggested we set up a game of Crown and Anchor to separate them from a bit of it. The officers had planned a camp concert in a couple of days and that seemed a good time to do it, so we showed Slim how to play on a board that George drew in the dirt with his finger. The beauty of Crown and Anchor is that if there are enough players to cover the whole board, the bank takes enough on every roll of the dice to cover any winnings. To that end George left it up to Slim and his wondrous powers of persuasion to convince the Texans we were 'on the level'.

Before the big day, Jimmy and a mate went out on a work detail and came back with two tins of bully beef they 'found' on the wharf. Back in camp for *tenko*, little Jimmy stood on the tins of beef in the back row and managed to get them in without being caught by the Japanese. But one of our officers saw him walking in with the beef under his arms and accused him of stealing them from stores. The officer reported it to the Japanese who put both Jimmy and his mate in solitary confinement in the 'chook shed', not much more than a lean-to, out in the sun for fourteen days. We never tolerated theft by one of our own and Jimmy's name became mud overnight. Sublieutenant Stone did a little asking around and told us that Jimmy was innocent, someone had 'crossed their wires', and when Jimmy got out of solitary he might have to be sent to another camp. The brass didn't want anyone 'having a go' at him for no good reason.

It turned out to be very competitive to get on work parties, even the officers had a hard time managing it, but Slim's money came in useful to bribe the guards and we were often chosen. We'd march to Batavia's main harbour at Tanjung Priok and work in the warehouses on the wharves. We'd been there not long before, but under different circumstances. The harbour was now filled with shipping. The Japs would take out local Javanese on lighters to salvage what they could from the bombed ships. We loaded warehouses with whatever the Japs found and kept a certain amount for ourselves; it was rich pickings. We did our best to help the war effort by sabotaging any recovered equipment or dropping important parts into

Jimmy's strange encounter in the sorting shed

the harbour. Little luxuries we found, like pencils, paper or food, we stole a little at a time. We learned if we distracted the guards with jokes we could slip things into baggy shorts for the trip back to camp. The Dutch women would toss fruit to us, and the guards often threatened them but never did anything. We had no way of knowing then, but when we left the Bicycle Camp those same women and their children would take our place as POWs.

George Grieve had one of *Perth*'s signalmen, Yeoman Jack Willis, paint a rice bag with the traditional Crown and Anchor board so it could be folded and hidden. The bag was a work of art, with beautifully painted symbols and an elaborate border design of sea creatures wound about heavy rope. We made a deal with the master-at-arms: half the money we won at Crown and Anchor would go into the ratings' mess fund because they had very little, while our officers got paid ten times more than we did to supply the Japanese with POW labour and never worked themselves. That was their deal with the Japs.

The time came for the concert and a chance to make some US dollars from the Texans. The men who organised the concert did a terrific job with coloured bunting, and Lucky Lasslett ran around with his bandana wound around his head arranging the lights. He carried on as he had at the cinema when we moved to the Bicycle Camp; neither our officers nor the Japs ever challenged him or said anything about it so he kept at it.

Our first concert meant a big effort from our cooks, who sold satay sticks rumoured to be made from cats caught on the wharves, but they did a roaring trade anyway. Some American sailors from the *Houston* set up a stand selling tinned milk flavoured with fruit or coconut and served in your own dixie. We went early to set up the Crown and Anchor game on a table that George scrounged from the mess hall, and we pooled our money for the bank. There was already a game of two-up underway with a lot of Yanks playing, so to attract them to our table I rolled the dice and Slim shouted every time he won – he always won – and that soon got their attention. Some Aussies who knew the game also drifted over and helped cover the table, and the house won money on every throw of the dice. In an hour and a half we'd won a mound of US dollars and a large tin full of coins. When time came for the concert we rolled up the game and made our way inside the hall, where the Japs sat in front-row seats.

Among the Australian POWs we had concert and opera singers, radio announcers, actors and a lot of pretty 'actresses'. The Japanese loved seeing men dressed as girls, a specialised art in Japan. We used instruments left by the Dutch, and our musicians, some from town bands and others professionals, played superbly. Some of our songs were rewritten because they would insult those Japanese who knew English. The costumes were made by professional tailors, and the 'showgirls' got plenty of wolf-whistles and shouts from the captive audience, with blokes yelling out, 'I'll see you after the show, luvvie.' Some songs from home brought silence and tears.

At show's end, the performers took their bows and the Jap officers stood and clapped, handing out cigarettes and lollies to each 'girl'. After the concert we thought we'd try our luck again with the Crown and Anchor game until two AIF officers demanded twenty per cent of the take for their mess. When we declined, the buggers said they would get the guards to close us down. We'd made a quid and decided we were way ahead of the game so quickly packed up, giving the ratings' mess their share and stashing the profits in a few different hidey-holes.

Next morning the guards carried out a search, lashed into a few blokes who put up resistance and eventually found our board and dice and money tins, but not our profits. We noticed the Japs never stole personal items and preferred trading things like military buttons, badges or watches, otherwise useless to the owners. These guards took what they found. Slim complained to an already furious Yank colonel about the rogue guards, who complained in turn to the commandant, and a few hours later we all got our money tins back, but not the Crown and Anchor dice or the painted mat. The commandant considered the Crown and Anchor mat contraband and, more to the point, a work of art, which it was, and he kept it. The two AIF officers who dobbed us in copped a severe talking-to from Brigadier Blackburn, the senior Australian officer in camp, and that made us all feel a little better.

The Japs set up a bulletin board with sanitised news dealing with Japanese and Axis victories and I read it as part of my daily routine. One day there was an offer for Australians to send a message home via the Japanese radio to be broadcast by Rohan Rivett, an Australian journalist in the camp who had worked for the Malayan Broadcasting Commission. The message had to be limited to just our name and home town. Men lined up all night for the chance and I was one of the lucky ones. The radio signal was strong in Western Australia and a Perth woman heard the broadcast and noted as much information as she could, then wrote letters to the parents stating what she heard. I could only imagine how my parents in Byron Bay felt getting their first news that I was still alive. It would be another twelve months before they got another word.

When the US Navy destroyed two Imperial Japanese Navy aircraft carrier fleets in the Coral Sea in May 1942 it probably saved Australia from invasion, but from that moment onwards the attitude of our guards changed towards us; they became more aggressive and taunted us. Very few POWs knew that we had a radio in camp but the commandant must have suspected it, and early one morning his soldiers turned the camp upside down looking until they found one, immediately beheading the Australian who had it. That shocked us and for a few days we lay low.

The Japanese filled the camp bulletin board with propaganda whenever the fortunes of war went in their favour and even posted news of Rommel's gains in Egypt and North Africa. We read the bulletins but yearned for news of the Allies retaking Java and freeing us. As time went on some of the men became more and more disappointed, especially the older men who wanted to believe we'd soon be going home. I always thought it was better to avoid being let down and never got my hopes up too much or let myself get too low.

From the secret radios we had heard that the Japs were having a hard time in New Guinea. This was the first time that they had lost forward momentum. Our food rations were cut suddenly and any complaints about it went unanswered. We quickly lost condition and, to make matters worse, the Japanese guards bashed us for little things like sitting on beds during the day, not saluting properly or not standing to attention when they passed. Our officers warned us to keep 'a weather eye' and avoid getting bashed; they suspected the Japanese were getting bad news from the front. Rumours sprang up and did the rounds of the camp in minutes, and then another would start and then another. Only one rumour turned out to be on the money: we were told that we had to sign a pledge of allegiance to the Imperial Japanese Army or face execution. Signing that pledge also meant we had to respect Japanese regulations as if we were part of their army. Naturally our officers refused so no one would sign it. The commandant assembled the inmates, had his men separate our officers from the enlisted men, and then said the officers would be staked to the ground in the sun and be the first to die unless the entire camp signed. Our CO, Brigadier Blackburn, decided the Japs were fair dinkum and saw no point in needless deaths and any further resistance; he ordered every man in the camp to sign. We did as ordered. It humiliated every one of us and never sat right.

Slim brought a few of his shipmates from the USS *Houston* to our barracks and we had some fun with them, telling them tall tales about kangaroos hopping over the Harbour Bridge, even though they had been to Sydney. We told them they had to be up early to see the wildlife and they never knew if we were serious or not. One sailor complained about having a pile of dollars but nothing to buy, probably a very silly thing to say to the Australians, and word got around quickly, so a few enterprising types set up a night market in our barracks. It resembled a native village with a few stalls, nothing too organised, it just happened. Two blokes with a camp stove bought eggs 'through the wire' from villagers and fried them in palm oil, charging punters a 200 per cent mark-up. Another bloke sketched portraits for a decent fee, and one sailor cut fencing wire into small bits to sell as flint replacements for the Americans' Zippo lighters. I suppose if you have little, you improvise. The Yanks knew we were making money but they were very good to us, and even let us believe we were getting the better of them. Slim told us they didn't mind paying; they hadn't anything else to do with their cash but spend it. In any case, what they spent with us we would likely spend with them, one way or another.

After three weeks I finally caught up with my mate Jimmy, who filled me in about the bully beef incident and his time in solitary in the chook shed. I somehow knew he'd never steal from his mates; he was just unlucky. At the end of his sentence some AIF officers arranged for Jimmy and fourteen others to be sent to work on an inland tobacco farm for three weeks. Jimmy said it was like a holiday for them and their three guards. There were no young men on the farm, just elderly men and women and some children. The able-bodied men from the village worked in Batavia gathering orders to keep the farm busy, a tidy and profitable business for the camp commandant who pushed off the Dutch farmer and kept the farm as his private little earner. The local farmhands had worked for Dutch farmers most of their lives but most were now in their twilight years, and picking and processing tobacco leaf in the heat was beyond them. Apparently they cheered when told the POWs would harvest their crop. The guards and locals joked among themselves as they watched the prisoners working in the heat, just like they had worked for the Dutch; it amused them to the extent that they sometimes doubled over laughing. Jimmy said he didn't mind, it was better than a jab in the ribs with a rifle butt, and mostly he enjoyed being out of the Bicycle Camp.

The farmhands showed Jimmy the technique of sorting harvested leaf, then bundling and hanging it on drying racks.

It wasn't the hardest job and he had time to have a good look around in relative freedom. He loved the flat, rich land in Java and how it reminded him of the cane fields of North Queensland. Before he joined the army, he'd sailed out of Cairns on the RMS *Aorangi* for the Union Steam Ship line and had always wanted to go back up there and start a tobacco farm of his own. On the farm, a Dutch colonist in his work party translated for the Dutch woman who managed it. She said after the next harvest she and her two teenage daughters would be interned in a civilian camp. Jimmy, a sympathetic type, shared whatever supplies he had with her and she in turn brought the workers food, her two buxom daughters helping to serve. Jimmy was a shy bloke, short and not much to him, but his blue eyes and easy smile probably made him attractive to the girls, though he would have been the last to know. When he came back from his 'holiday' he told us a story, but warned us that we probably wouldn't believe him.

'One of the girls was about seventeen or eighteen and she always gave me a smile when she gave me my grub.' We were sceptical. 'Next day I ran out of tobacco sacks and went out the back to the sorting shed to get some more and found her there. She gave me a funny look, unbuttoned her blouse and exposed two white melons with pennies stuck on the end of each.'

'Then what did you do?'

'I grabbed more bags and went back to work.'

'Bullshit.'

'I told you you wouldn't believe me.'

We had a good laugh about that and it became a useful distraction for us in the coming weeks, and it was much better than crying. Jimmy brought back a 'swag' bulging with prime tobacco leaves and said he could probably get more. The farmhands had shown him how to rub the cured tobacco leaf in the palm of his hands and chop it up to roll a decent cigarette. He made a few and handed them around. Slim picked one, smelled it, lit up and, deciding they were pretty good, said he would get top dollar from the Texans. Jimmy was happy for Slim to do the business and they deposited quite a few dollars in our 'bank'.

Slim liked Jimmy and wanted to know how we met. I told him I grew up in Byron Bay in northern New South Wales, a shipping port for local dairy and pork produce. I worked in Anderson's Piggery, delivering smallgoods to the wharf, while Jimmy worked on the SS *Wollongbar*, which regularly sailed between Sydney and Byron Bay carrying smallgoods, dairy products and timber as well as passengers, and we met often at dockside. Watching the *Wollongbar* leave port gave me the idea that I wanted to join the navy one day and see the world, and when the war began I signed up.

Not long after Jimmy's return from the tobacco farm I suffered my first bout of malaria and spent a week in the camp hospital under the care of our doctor, Lieutenant Colonel EE

'Weary' Dunlop. He looked after me and all the other sick men very well, walking through the ward every day and speaking to us as equals.

After my discharge I immediately felt a different atmosphere in the camp: supplies were shorter, ration portions had been reduced substantially and Korean guards had replaced the Japanese. We called the Koreans 'duck shooters' because of the way they nursed their rifles. We heard that the Japanese guards were being sent as troops to the front line for the invasion of Australia. The idea of a Japanese invasion was the nightmare we all feared.

Because food was now in short supply we depended more on men buying 'through the wire' from the locals and paying with Japanese occupation script, but the locals didn't want a bar of it. They only wanted precious US dollars, so our cooks used leftover rice to brew rice wine, which they sold to the Americans at a good profit. We converted those dollars into anything we could buy outside. That all came to an end when the rice was needed for the Japanese troops and we had barely enough to eat, let alone convert into wine. Our head cook was a canny lad who bought any fresh food he could from the camp canteen or through the wire from the local natives, but the newly arrived Korean guards taxed him for a share. The cook complained to Brigadier Blackburn, who immediately took the complaint to the camp commandant and, for the first time, nothing came of it. Something was in the wind. Another rumour swirled around and around: our commandant would soon be shipped out to the front and lose all his perks *and* his tobacco farm. The Japanese posted on the bulletin board that their troops were quickly marching towards victory, and that raised the anxiety level all around. We had nothing but time to think and talk and imagine what might be happening. We still had two radios from which we learned some things, but never everything and never enough.

Our commandant's replacement was Lieutenant Suzuki, and his arrival confirmed the rumour. He decided to show more care towards his POWs, getting the Australian and American commanders together and proposing a series of sporting events, beginning with volleyball, boxing and tug-o'-war. The first event, volleyball, proved to be a good diversion and the whole camp watched. We had no idea of the finer points of the game but some *Houston* survivors trained our navy blokes on the quiet. One of our blokes kept a book and made the Yanks short favourites, and they beat us pretty easily. The bookie also started a buzz that the *Perth* tug-o'-war team was the fleet champion, so the Yanks heavily backed the Aussies for the win, but somehow the Yanks won that as well with dollars changing hands, some of them ours; it was rumoured that some of the Aussie tug-o'-war team backed the Yanks.

That night in a carnival atmosphere we waited for the boxing to start while blokes played two-up in the barracks, and the food stands made a motza. Japanese officers and Korean guards turned out and clapped and cheered after each exhibition, throwing sweets instead of money into the ring and lifting camp morale immensely. The boxing was well attended and the Australian team held its own. Suzuki was so impressed he wanted to organise a touring troupe for exhibitions outside. Our officers were all for it and even convinced Suzuki that to ensure good contests the men needed more food. He agreed to the extra rations, which were immediately put into the camp pool and shared equally, and that was also very good for camp morale.

One morning several West Australians were rounded up and mustered into the administration building, which started rumours flying. The one I recall was that Western Australia was leaving the Commonwealth and joining the Imperial Japanese Forces and siding with the Emperor. It was such a wild idea that some West Australians believed it and thought that they were about to be sent home. The Japanese intelligence officers set up clearly marked maps of Western Australia showing seaports, towns, rivers, bridges, railway lines and roads and asked the men to give detailed information on each point of the map.

One West Australian, Blood Bancroft, told me about it. 'The Japanese in charge spoke perfect English, told me to sit and pointed at the top of the West Australian map with a cane and wanted to know what was there. I was from Perth and had never been outside of Perth and I told him so. He asked me again and I said I had no idea. Then he whacked my collarbone with the cane. I don't know why, but I didn't like being spoken to the way he went about it and I said my school teacher hit harder than he did and she was a woman. He went red in the face and then lost his bundle and screamed for the Korean guard, who knocked me to the floor. The officer screamed again and they put me back in the chair. The officer had a bad lisp and I thought of imitating him but decided against it.'

I had a laugh listening to him and he went on. 'He said if I gave untruthful answers he would chop off my head and I believed him. I tell you, the Japanese must have had spies on the pearl luggers off Broome mapping the towns and roads because he knew more about the northern parts of Western Australia than I ever did. They knew where the major roads, rivers and bridges and the major railway junctions were, as well as big towns and small towns. I didn't fancy losing my head for knowing nothing so I just nodded when he told me anything. Afterwards an officer debriefed me and it became clear that the Japanese invasion of Australia was still early in the planning stage.' That bit of intelligence relieved us all.

The Japanese allowed the Koreans to brutalise us, and those buggers needed little encouragement. One Korean guard, a brute we called Dogface, beat anyone if they didn't salute properly whenever a Jap officer was around. When the whole camp was called out to the parade ground and the

Korean guards patrolled, they hit anyone found sitting due to malnutrition or the heat. Our officers warned us to not give the Koreans any excuse. In contrast, the Japs performed acts of kindness for the camp inmates, so we wouldn't know from day to day if we were Arthur or Martha.

Brigadier Blackburn called us to assemble for parade before three senior Japanese officers on the Emperor's birthday, which we were to celebrate with them. 'On this grand occasion, we show you the power and might of Imperial Japan.' We heard a rumble and a formation of Japanese bombers and fighter planes flew low overhead; the ground shook. Jap officers shouted, 'Banzai! Banzai! Banzai!' Our officers were told to salute the flight above, and that the planes were on their way to bomb Australia; that sent shudders throughout the ranks. Then the Japanese officer announced that a fairly big quantity of Australian flour of unknown origin would be given to the camp cooks to bake fresh bread for everyone, and that brought a cheer, which impressed the Japs. We couldn't understand them: they were going to bomb Australia as soon as they could but we'd get fresh baked bread.

Knowing we had nothing to bake it in, some of the men, brickies in civilian life, got to work and jerry-built a brick oven, ripping out bricks from every second building pier. The result was an odd-looking affair but in the next days the aroma of fresh-baked bread filled the camp, for most of us our first bread in six months.

The Japs also let each man write a Red Cross card home; we were only allowed to say that we were POWs and that the Japanese were treating us very well.

After that little episode, however, morale sank to its lowest with no good news or even decent rumours, and everything started to go downhill in the Bicycle Camp. The men continually lost weight and our clothes began rotting in the humidity. One of the *Perth* men, a sail-maker, made a killing mending the clothes we had but, even so, most of us went back to wearing the G-string. Some officers organised an arts and craft show to raise morale and keep us busy. Ray Parkin, a talented artist from the *Perth*, displayed his paintings and even sold some to the Japanese. Many men in our camp had real talents, but it all went to waste on our journey as prisoners of war.

When we first entered the Bicycle Camp some of our men admired the Japs for their courage and efficiency. They slowly changed their minds after the Japs cut rations and ignored our privations, our conditions worsening by the day. Even going out to the wharves in work parties ceased being a picnic; the Korean guards became ever more vigilant and it was hard to smuggle anything into camp. Any men caught were first beaten then put in the chook shed for up to three weeks at a time. The Dutch women who used to slip us fruit or cakes had disappeared and we were forced to work longer hours on the wharves, loading rice crops and machinery to be shipped back to Japan. I secretly hoped our submarines were active and ensuring this stuff was not making it through.

On 11 October 1942, after eight months in captivity, we were told we would be leaving the Bicycle Camp next morning, all 1200 Australian, American and Dutch POWs. We had no idea where we were going or how, but the cooks worked all night preparing boiled rice to take on the journey. Survivors of the *Perth* and *Houston* had been through it all before but this was the first time for our army mates. We had very few possessions to take, although the medical staff managed to smuggle out some hidden medical equipment.

Tenko for over 1200 men took three attempts in the heat, but finally the count produced a satisfactory result and the men grew restless. Rumours flew about our destination as idle minds worked: we were going home after a prisoner swap; we were going to Sumatra or Japan or Banka Island. You believed what you wanted, but the sad truth of it is that two men, in despair, committed suicide. After what we went through I gave up listening to invented stories, but lots of money was wagered on our destination. I never heard if any were proved right.

This time there was no marching for us; a train pulled up hauling dozens of cattle cars. It was a short distance back to the wharf but it took ages to get there, and when we did the smell of the sea was almost too much for the men who had not worked at the harbour; they'd forgotten what it was like. The train stopped at the wharf and we marched onto a dock alongside the *Kinkon Maru*, an ageing rust bucket that did not look big enough to take us all in its dirty hold. The smell below decks sickened us, but even in all that mess some men still placed bets as to our destination.

George, Slim, Jimmy and I stayed together while the ship remained tied up until next morning. The cooks on board fed us a watery vegetable soup and our dixies came in handy; the blokes who'd left theirs behind to bring other possessions soon realised their mistake. None of us would lend ours owing to the chance of disease that floated around, and it's hard to eat soup with your hands. Latrines were set up on the main deck, two pieces of timber stuck over the side, and we had fun watching our army mates straddle them while holding a length of rope to stop them falling into the water. The Jap captain allowed us to wash under a fire hose, sea water only. It served two purposes: one to wash and the other to keep the deck cool. It was still hot, sweaty and stinking in the hold and the guards left us alone.

Early next morning we felt the engines starting, and as we pulled out of harbour one of our senior officers suggested to the captain that we paint 'POW' on each side of the ship, but he would not be in it. The ship sat very low in the water and made about eight knots an hour at best, an easy target for any of the American, British and Dutch submarines active in the area. We'd heard about them on our last remaining radio and those in the know became very nervous about our voyage. At times, whenever the ship zigzagged violently, the hold went deathly silent; we'd stare at one another and some men prayed while others told jokes. We all feared being torpedoed.

Somehow the element of chance played its hand and we ran the gauntlet safely, and after three days some men using the *benjo* up on deck saw land on the horizon. When we got closer someone recognised it as the Singapore Roads strait, the main shipping lane into Keppel Harbour, and the lights of the city shone brightly in the distance. The ship started to slow, then we heard the anchor rattling out, and finally the engines stopped. There was utter silence for the first time in three days. We swung at anchor until the morning when the captain allowed groups topside for a breath of fresh air, a few hundred men at a time. I got out on the fourth outing and treasured the cool morning. If I closed my eyes I could be wherever I wanted, if only for half an hour.

The guards held the men back in the overheated hold and recriminations started up, stories flying back and forth. There was a buzz that before we left the Bicycle Camp some officers bought most of the canned food left in the canteen. It proved to be right when we saw the weight of their kitbags. Even our own officers shunned them. They never left their kitbags unattended. I know what would have happened if they did. We just wanted to survive, but those blokes had no honour. The smell of distant cooking blew gently over us from the city, some good, some not so good, but at least the smells were free as far as we could tell. We tried to guess what was cooking but few of us had any idea about Asian food.

Late in the morning a tug escorted the *Kinkon Maru* through the minefields, sampans, motor launches and Jap submarine hunters crisscrossing the harbour. Once it was tied up on the dock, the gangway went into place and we assembled on the wharf for the inevitable *tenko*, and once again the Japs came up short. We were going through it for the second time when one of our doctors told the guards that three men had died below decks. Everyone was glad to be off that ship, but none more so than our army mates.

Chapter 4

On the wharf were rows of Australian army trucks with the rising sun painted on their bonnets. We could see Australian diggers wearing their slouch hats working on the wharf in the distance, but they were too far away for a talk so we just waved. Most of us had never been to Singapore before and while we waited to be loaded onto the trucks one of the Yanks pointed out Raffles Hotel and the Johor Bahru Bridge to Malaya. With no warning a Korean guard bashed him with a rifle butt and shouted, 'No talk.' We had nicknames for most of the Korean guards and that one we called the 'Brown Bomber' because he went off like a bomb. The Yank collapsed and the guards would not let anyone touch him until one of the Yank medics appeared. Later in the war we heard stories of MV *Krait* dropping commandoes into Singapore to plant limpet mines on Japanese shipping, and we always hoped that the Brown Bomber was on one of the many ships sunk.

Before boarding the trucks we were searched again, and this time we did the double-shuffle with the medical equipment and other contraband. We had learned how to smuggle items under slouch hats or turbans, and all kinds of things, including a radio and power for it, disappeared and reappeared as if by magic. I only carried my dixie, a spoon, my money tin, a skinny blanket and Knocka White's watch – all I had. The loading of the men onto the trucks went slowly and we heard that a couple of pistols were pushed through the cracks in the wharf and into the drink; I don't know how true that is but their owners took a terrible risk.

We were driven through the streets of Singapore and saw people going about their daily lives, no attention directed towards us, and saw few signs of the destruction we expected. We did see a couple of British work parties clearing some bomb-damaged buildings and some of our men called out and they waved back, but that was as close as we came to them.

The trucks drove the length of the island and eventually pulled up outside a large arched gate with one word lettered on it: Changi. That name meant nothing to us. Our Korean guards from the Bicycle Camp waited outside for the camp guards while the inmates came to greet the new arrivals, standing on the other side of the fence and staring at us as we sat in the trucks. We must have looked a sight in our tattered rags and G-strings. We were so used to the sight of each other that we were surprised at the reaction of the Changi inmates, some shedding tears. They asked us who we were.

'We're Aussies from the *Perth* and Yanks from the *Houston* and 131st Field Regiment.'

They said nothing else as they looked at us half-living scarecrows. I remember George saying we didn't look too bad, but by contrast these blokes looked fit, healthy and well fed, all the officers dressed in proper kit right down to swagger sticks and polished Sam Browne belts.

The Korean guard we called Dogface, an unpleasant little fellow, started a shouting match with the Jap guards and got a severe dressing-down; they belittled him and made him bow low. Those little details showed us their pecking order and gave us an insight into Jap culture. They never let the Koreans forget their place and they treated prisoners with less contempt than the Koreans. Apparently this had gone on for hundreds of years. We could never work out the Japanese.

We couldn't believe how good our men looked, with nicely ironed uniforms and polished boots. We even saw a game of Aussie Rules football taking place in the distance. One of our men took a keen interest, as it was rumoured he was a champion player from Subiaco in Perth. They called him 'Blood' – short for Bloodnut – Bancroft, a redhead and no apologies. Slim smiled when we explained the nickname, shaking his head; he didn't know much about Aussie slang then but he'd soon learn.

We waited in the trucks outside the front gate of Changi for a few hours, then the trucks started up again and drove away. We were used to disappointment so nothing surprised us, and half an hour later we'd decided that the Koreans were lost until we pulled up at another gate. This time we were expected; we saw a dozen immaculately dressed Australian and British officers standing at ease with swagger sticks under their arms. They looked very pukka, dressed in tropical rig: shorts and long socks with polished boots. Changi was not one camp but seven, occupying the peninsula at the eastern end of Singapore Island, so no wonder the Koreans got confused.

We were ordered off the trucks for our usual *tenko* then made to stand in formation next to the Texan Artillery and the *Houston* survivors. At best we were a motley-looking group, some men dressed in the remnants of their kit and wearing their G-strings as turbans. Brigadier Blackburn called us to attention and we tried very hard to do the right thing by him, even though we no longer looked like seamen and soldiers.

'Parade, right turn, parade, quick march, parade, eyes *righttt!*' The brigadier took the salute and we marched into our new camp under the gaze of Australian and British officers.

One said, 'They look like rabble.' We adopted that name as a de facto badge of honour, and from then on we were the Java Rabble, under the command of Major Weary Dunlop, after Brigadier Blackburn was transferred from Changi to Manchuria, and very proud of it.

Changi had been a British Army base. With the sea as a backdrop behind swaying palm trees, it looked like a postcard. On our way in we saw men playing tennis and walking around freely, reading books or working in a chook shed and a large vegetable garden. Compared to the Bicycle Camp this place looked like 'a piece of heaven', as one of our men said. We were sent to Selarang Barracks: neat rows of well-constructed accommodation and shower blocks assembled in an open area.

With hundreds of men to process quickly, the Australian Army took over; they separated the Americans and marched them off to their own orientation. For his own reasons, Slim decided to stay with us. The Australian officers went to the officers' mess and our sick went to the hospital, where they were well treated by good doctors armed with potent drugs and medicines. Chief petty and petty officers were singled out and their details entered in the camp ledgers, then off they went to their barracks. That done, the army at last took our details – name, rank and number – and had us fill out next-of-kin cards. It took hours, and when they finished the paperwork they showed us to our accommodation.

Compared to the steel plate of a rusty transport ship or the concrete floor of the cinema, it was luxury. The army treated us kindly and did a thorough job assigning us cots in barracks. They issued each man a towel, soap and razors to be shared and gave men wearing G-strings new shorts and a shirt. Boots were in short supply and most of us went barefoot, except for some men who wore sandals that had been made by a Dutch POW who did a non-stop trade in the Bicycle Camp until caught by the Japs leaving one night to visit his wife, and we

The rabble arrives

never saw him again. At long last, paperwork and handouts over, we lined up to stand under our first freshwater shower after a week spent mostly stuck in a ship's hold.

After ablutions we marched to the mess, just as we had in Recruit School, and met some *Houston* survivors, now dressed in Aussie khaki shorts and shirts; it was hard to tell them from us. The army cooks had prepared a welcoming meal of beef stew and vegetables, unimaginable just moments before. Soldiers waited tables laden with fresh bread and cordial, and to cap off a bon-ton feed they brought out duff and tinned peaches with custard, like our mums used to make, our best meal in eight months. That really hit us for six; some men wept. Chaplain Mathieson walked from table to table talking to our men. He still wore the gear Slim had given him in the cinema weeks before, and when he saw Slim he said the clothes were 'wearing well'.

'My pleasure, sir,' Slim said and shook his hand.

'You're a good man. And how are you, Stoker Munro?'

'I'm well, thanks to my good mates, sir.' I put my arm around George.

'Well, look after the baby,' the chaplain told George. Everyone called me the baby, although I no longer looked eighteen or felt it.

A few weeks before our arrival, Red Cross parcels had landed in Singapore and most of the contents were already distributed, but the army men freely shared their allotted cigarettes. An American officer came and spoke to Slim and took him away.

'I'll see you guys later,' he said.

In 1942 we were around 15,000 Australians in Changi and there were many unexpected reunions. A *Perth* sailor met his two brothers who he thought were still in Australia, and I met Daniel Baker from Murwillumbah, who I'd gone to school with in Mullumbimby. Through Daniel I met his mate Freddie Fuggle, from Sydney, and a bunch of their army cobbers. Everyone had their story and they always wanted to hear yours. We sat around in the shade of a tree and swapped tales.

I told Daniel Baker and his mates about the sinking of the *Perth* and they chorused 'Christ' and 'Bugger me' at every twist and turn. I also told them about losing my new boots and they had a good laugh. I always tried to keep it light, so finished my tale by describing the *benjo* on transport ships and how undignified and dangerous using it was, and how Wireman Lucky Lasslett became the camp electrician. We swapped snippets of news from home but I kept my feelings and the news from our radio to myself. I had learned it was best to keep mum and tried never to listen to rumours, but from what they said it sounded like the army blokes had their own radio in Changi.

Compared to the inmates of Changi, the Java Rabble were dead easy to spot among the camp population. With our oil-stained skin, deep suntans and hollow cheeks, we stood out like skeletons; the army blokes could barely look at us. Changi was a huge place of twenty-odd acres with dozens of solid buildings and so, with nothing much else to do, we explored. Walking around one day I saw a sign saying 'Library' and entered, intent on getting something to read to alleviate the boredom. An Indian guard stopped me and pointed at another sign: 'Officers Only'. He smiled, tipping his head left and right a few times, and I left. I couldn't believe we had Indian Army soldiers guarding us with rifles, but they were far more civil to us than the Koreans and we never had problems with them. We learned that the Japs had convinced the Indians that Japan would win the war, and when they did they would kick out the remnants of British rule and allow the Indians self-determination, something that Gandhi had wanted for years. The Indians guarding us must have taken the Japanese at their word, but these same blokes later died in the Burmese jungle for those beliefs.

There were a lot of different activities taking place in the camp. We passed a group of soldiers dressed for the beach and asked what was going on. They told us Adrian Curlewis, a famous lifesaver, was giving a lifesaving course. There was another group of men sitting on chairs practising speaking like Pommies. We thought that was funny. Daniel Baker told us the teacher, Alec Downer, was from South Australia and his father used to be premier of the state. He thought we should be able to speak better so was giving elocution lessons.

George, Jimmy and I stuck together like we had in the Bicycle Camp and exercised regularly by walking the perimeter of our area. Along the way we'd often run into Daniel, Freddie Fuggle and their army mates. We'd sit under a shade tree and talk, their sergeant telling us once this story about their capture in Singapore.

'We had no idea how to fight the Nips. They formed little attack parties in the jungle instead of having one front. They rode pushbikes on paths they'd cut and sneaked up on our units, annihilating our men one at a time. We kept losing men and falling back, and towards the end we were no longer one big army. Most of our officers were dead and we scattered into ragtag units which the Japanese exploited, and we lost many more. Two weeks before the Japs bombed Singapore, a division of Pommy troops arrived and we hoped the extra manpower would help us turn the Japs back, but the Poms weren't acclimatised, and they were unprepared for the onslaught and next to useless. Many were staff, not front line, and they hadn't fired a gun since Recruit School. Since our air force had been shot out of the sky, it was bloody mayhem and the Japs pushed through and captured over 100,000 troops. Some of our high brass got away but the rest surrendered and were forced to pass over their side-arms to the Japanese as part of the official surrender – a final act of humiliation in front of the lined-up soldiers. Then the buggers made us line the roads and watch the Imperial Japanese Army march past while Japanese propaganda photographers set up cameras and filmed the proceedings for those back home.'

George mentioned to the sergeant that in the chaos in Java there were many men with no officers or orders who were branded as deserters. The sergeant explained they weren't deserters at all but remnants of isolated units ordered to get out of Singapore as best they could. Some got as far as Java before their capture. Some senior officers, we heard, even got home to Australia before the Japanese occupation.

'What about escaping?' George asked.

The sergeant replied, 'That would be the easy part, but there is nowhere to escape to. There've been a lot who tried and they're all dead and buried. The Malays were ruled by the British since it was discovered by Raffles and they see the Japs as liberators who reward them for siding with them. Some blokes slip out at night to buy whatever they can from the Chinese, and we can trust them because they hate the Japs because of what they did in Nanking. Do you know what happened in Nanking?'

We didn't.

'They raped and murdered over 200,000 Chinese and they could easily do that to us in here.'

We thought about that while puffing on our smokes and staring into space for a while.

'How long were you on the *Perth*, George?' the sergeant asked.

'Six months. I served on the HMAS *Vendetta,* part of the Scrap Iron Flotilla, and I joined *Perth* when I got back from the Mediterranean. I admired the *Perth* when I first saw her in Alexandria and never thought I'd get a draft to her.'

'You poor bastard,' the sergeant said. 'You blokes sure get to see the world. What about you, Stoker?'

'*Perth* was my first ship. I joined up when I was seventeen, just after I left school. Daniel Baker and I went to school in Mullumbimby together and this is the last place I ever expected to see him.'

'Me too,' said Daniel. It gave us a laugh.

'It's pretty easy in here, plenty of good food. Some blokes started a school, and in the Pommy section they play soccer at a pretty high level, as some of their blokes played first grade. But I have to tell you boys, there is one place you should steer clear of.' The sergeant started to giggle. 'It's the place where the poofters gather at night.'

I burst out laughing. 'Which nights?'

'Where do they meet?' asked George.

'Down behind the canteen. They're alright, just a bit queer that's all, and they always have cigarettes and something good to eat, and if you make them laugh they'll share it with you. It's not compulsory to join them, but they're all good blokes.'

George said that at sea in the RAN it is a mortal sin for sailors to 'cross the line'; if they do they are tossed off the ship straight away.

We said our farewells to the army boys and headed back to our mess for dinner. When we got back to our barracks we saw that most of our men were missing, cots stripped and gear gone. A petty officer saw us standing around looking bewildered.

'Where have you lot been?'

George, always quick on his feet, said, 'Jimmy's coming down with malaria. We took him to the camp hospital.'

The PO knew we were having him on. 'I suppose you lot know nothing about the missing chickens from the officers' chicken coop?'

'No, Petty Officer. I hope you don't think we took them. We just got here so it was probably the army blokes, but if you give us a couple of days, we'll get the rest.'

The PO took a long look at us; we looked like we could do with a good feed but we hadn't any need to knock off a few chooks, as the army mess fed us well.

'You cheeky buggers. Get your gear, you're being moved to new quarters. Be back here in twenty minutes with your belongings.'

Our belongings didn't amount to much – one blanket, one mosquito net, shorts and shirt, a G-string and a cigarette tin. We mustered outside with other Java men and marched to our new accommodation in Changi. The new quarters were as good as the last, but far from the chicken coops. I immediately missed the views of the sea and the sunsets and the tropical palms. Slim turned up that night carrying his belongings and pulled out another bottle of bourbon that he was pleased to let us help drink. He told us that we would not be there long, that was all. We'd learned not to ask too many questions but he always seemed to know everything before anyone else. It was the last thing we wanted to hear; to us Changi was like a holiday camp. A few days later the Japanese forbade the *Perth* survivors going out on work parties, depriving us of the chance to get any contraband. Slim knew where the Chinese traders were and at night he went under the wire and brought us back fruit and cigarettes at cheaper prices than the canteen. We were soon to know officially why they were fattening us up.

November was fast approaching and the Australian high command wanted to hold a Melbourne Cup day. The Japs liked horseracing so they agreed to it. The organising committee set the rules. The horses were made up of a piece of wood with reins attached and the jockey held it between the legs. Each jockey wore a different colour and the idea was to get a bloke who could run. We elected Jimmy, about the right size and age to be a jockey, and made him our man.

'I'll be your trainer,' said George.

'I'll be your strapper,' I said.

'I'll be the owner,' said Slim.

'What else?' I said.

The bookies wandered around with watches in hand for the qualifying rounds and set the field. Poor old Jimmy didn't qualify, due, we reckoned, to his malaria. In any event, the first Tuesday in November 1942 turned out to be our best day in captivity. Some of the POWs dressed up with top hats made from cardboard and coloured with boot polish, and other blokes dressed up as fancy women to accompany the top-hatted gents. We invited Daniel Baker and Freddie Fuggle, just in case Slim had another bottle of bourbon whisky. After Jimmy failed in the qualifiers he joined us on the course. Doctors came, accompanied by men dressed as 'nurses', and heavily backed one of the Java Rabble: a tall, thin doctor who looked like he could leg it. The officers had their own favourite, a bloke who had once run in the Stawell Gift, a sprint over 115 yards. Our race was over 1500 yards but the officers ignored that fact and still backed their man. There were 25 'horses' entered, each with a name and wearing 'owner's colours'.

We pooled our money and backed our navy doctor, a sleeper at long odds, while the doctors and 'nurses' got stuck into their supply of medicinal brandy and got 'shickered'. The bookies wandered around shouting out the odds and collecting the bets. The army brass band played, adding to the atmosphere.

Patients from the hospital were wheeled out into the sunshine; cooks took time out from their pots and pans and came out dressed in their white aprons. The course was three laps of the open area between the barracks, with onlookers forming a wide circle. An official race caller, using a megaphone made from rolled-up paper, announced each runner, led by their strapper to the starting post, and everyone took their job seriously. The race announcer mounted an upturned box and raised the warning flag – a hush came over the crowd. He yelled, 'And they're off,' and down came the flag, the barefooted runners and their stick horses taking off to the sound of over 5000 men roaring as one. They roared so loudly it startled the Japs.

Every unit had a runner in the race and the crowd looked no different to any you'd expect to see at Flemington, except there were no pretty girls drinking champagne. The first time past the post, the officers' choice led the pack and they urged their runner on. The second time past the post the officers' choice had sprinted out too early and was beginning to lose puff; he was still in front but falling off the pace. The race caller announced that our doctor was making his way forward. And near the home turn our long-shot doctor pulled clear of the officers' choice and won in a canter. We cheered long and loudly, the doctors and 'nurses' screamed and the bookies grumbled; one up for the Java Rabble. Slim collected our winnings and returned much later with a bottle of spirits, and then we cheered some more.

Chapter 5

Our new accommodation in Changi was close to Daniel and Freddie's, and after our evening meal we celebrated our win. Slim cracked a bottle and poured each of us a share. It was not so much about the alcohol, but that night I completely forgot about our last eight months. It was a beautiful evening, each man had a full stomach, some decent liquor and friends to share it with and I've never forgotten it.

I overheard Daniel tell Slim what I was like back in Mullumbimby during our high school days. Just as I could not imagine Houston, Slim couldn't come to grips with Mullumbimby. Daniel told him that I was an avid rugby player, did fairly well at school, was a bit of a reader and that I never got into trouble, and he might have called me the teacher's pet except I was too big. That made Slim laugh. The truth is I never saw Daniel outside school because he lived 80 miles or so north of Mullumbimby in banana country and I lived in Byron Bay, so we caught different trains home. Daniel took a swig of bourbon and stared out into space; he just wanted to get back to his property in the Nightcap Ranges and tend his banana crop.

'What about you, Freddie? What would you like to do once this war is over?'

Freddie, a big lump of a bloke with curly hair, said, 'I'm going to join the police force. I want to help people.'

'How can you argue with that?' George responded. 'Cheers.'

Slim said, 'I've always wanted to say "Cheers" to you Aussies.'

'Well, cheers to you, Slim,' said George. We all drank to that and clanged our mugs.

'What about you, George, what do you want to do?' asked Slim.

'I want to go home to Zillmere in Brisbane with my Sydney-born wife, start an engineering shop, have some children and enjoy my life.' George's eyes glistened over as he told us about his wife. 'I'm married to the lovely Kathleen and I don't even have a photo of her. I met her at a dance at the Trocadero nightclub in Sydney. It was love at first sight. She worked at the post office and waited for me when we sailed to the Mediterranean. When I got home next the ship went into dry dock for a major refit, so we got married and bought a small place. After we had our honeymoon I returned to the *Vendetta*, then the navy said I was being promoted and had a draft to HMAS *Perth*. We'd decided, thank God, to wait till the war was over before starting a family.'

Tears streamed down his face so I put my arm around his shoulders and we had a bit of a cry. I thought of my parents and hoped they weren't worrying about me. Later on we made a promise that the first one home would telephone the other's parents. George's parents knew how to contact Kathleen. We swapped phone numbers and I memorised his parents' name and their address.

Slim asked Jimmy, 'What about you, mate?' Slim always said 'mate' in a Texan drawl; it sounded wrong, but Slim was the real article.

Jimmy said he wanted to go back to Cairns and farm tobacco. It was easy to grow and the Javanese had showed him the time-honoured way to get a good crop and handle the leaf properly. He reckoned the war had to be good for something, and that was what he had got out of it.

'What about you, Stoker?'

I looked at Slim and smiled. 'Why, I'm going to do what you did, Slim – stay in the navy because I love it, and I get to meet villains like you *and* travel the world.'

'Well, Stoker, if you ever get to Houston, come and see me. I'll be in the governor's mansion.'

'As his radio officer?'

'No, I'm a Texan, we think big. I want to be the governor.' As Aussies would, we all laughed at him.

The Japs treated us relatively well. They issued Red Cross cards to be filled in and sent to our next-of-kin. It gave us some hope that our loved ones at home would know we were alive. Apart from that card, I had no idea if the note I wrote in Java and Rohan Rivett's broadcast on radio ever reached my parents in Australia.

For some reason all full colonels and above were gathered together and transferred out of Changi. Slim, who knew everything, said they were being sent to Manchuria in China. The buzz was the Japs never wanted any high-ranking officers to see or hear what atrocities were to be inflicted on the men.

The senior Australian officer in Changi now was a lieutenant colonel – one step below a full colonel – 'Black Jack' Galleghan, who asked the Japs for permission to hold a march on Armistice Day, 11 November 1942. There was a bit of argy-bargy before he reminded the Japs that we fought alongside them in the Great War. Our army mates said Black Jack Galleghan had a fearsome reputation and the Japs would likely have been intimidated by him, and sure enough, they shortly gave permission.

Before the parade Jimmy got crook again with malaria and was back in hospital. A senior RAN officer planned the parade with the navy leading, as was proper; we were, after all, the senior service and, as tradition had it, always led military parades. Black Jack blew his stack. He was aware that almost the whole navy contingent was made up of the Java Rabble; none of us had boots, hats, shirts or navy-issue shorts. Some of us went barefoot or wore home-made sandals. At best we looked 'ragtag', exactly as our name suggested; our RAN officers were as poorly dressed as we were, and the navy blokes stood in contrast to the army POWs in their polished boots and uniforms pressed with the irons they had in their kits. But at last Black Jack grudgingly agreed. Navy officers sized us off

Armistice Day parade, 11 November 1942

and delivered a stirring speech to get us into the right frame of mind, asking us to put in our best effort. We tried, and in my opinion we looked pretty good. The band played and off we went. The order came for 'eyes right' and 500 heads turned as one to Black Jack on the podium, and our officers produced snappy salutes. The officers told us afterwards we'd done a good job and we were proud of ourselves; it was good for our morale.

Later we heard a buzz that Black Jack had questioned the way our officers saluted, and he was told the same story I had been in Recruit School. After the British fleet defeated the Spanish Armada, Queen Elizabeth I went to the wharf to thank the Royal Navy for saving England. When saluting her with their open palms, the sailors had showed blackened hands from the tarred lines and sheets of the sailing ships. So that she never saw their dirty hands in future, she officially changed the way the navy saluted to palms facing downwards, and the unsightly tarred palms were never shown again.

Slim delivered good news that meant more to us than a T-bone steak and chips with a schooner of beer. There had been a decisive blow to the Japs which he called the Battle of Midway. They had lost four aircraft carriers against the American Navy. It had happened five months ago in June, but old news was good news to us. The loss of the Jap ships meant further reducing the continuing risk of a Japanese invasion of Australia. The idea of Japan attacking Australia was finally put to bed for most of us and we breathed a collective sigh of relief.

Chapter 6

What really kept us going in Changi was sport. Nearly every day, there was some game on attracting big crowds, and it turned out to be a good place to meet English, Irish, Welsh, Scottish, Dutch and Indian POWs, as well as some of the American POWs we knew from Java. Bands played before and after matches and men set up stalls and sold all sorts of food. Some sold military insignia – divisional badges and medallions – to the Japs, who were very keen on them and paid well. We could even buy clothes, cigarettes singly or by the packet, and some enterprising blokes sold contraband under the counter, even bayonets and liquor. George and I took Slim along to one of the rugby union matches played between Australian medical staff and their British equivalents. With over 5000 spectators, the match was much better attended than we could have imagined. Black Jack and his staff officers plus their British counterparts lined up and shook hands with each of the players. At least 50 Jap officers sat in a specially constructed stand and apparently they loved rugby; they thought it was a bit like sumo wrestling. There was a rumour going around the game that the British team had a few all-England players in it. The Australian team had Major Weary Dunlop, a Wallaby and a proud member of the Java Rabble. As usual with games like this, the bookies were in attendance and they were big contributors to the camp fund.

From the kick-off the crowd didn't stop cheering. The Japs were very enthusiastic, more so than our officers who sat on their chairs and clapped politely, very 'rah-rah'. Slim wondered who the sergeant was sitting with our officers. I said it could be a batman, a soldier assigned to officers as a servant. I was more interested in the game and didn't take much interest.

'I don't think so,' said Slim. 'The officers are pouring him drinks.'

The game was heading for a draw and the British team attacked relentlessly. We had our backs against the wall and tackled ferociously, and the ball came loose; we got possession and Weary Dunlop beat their tired defence and ran over for the winning try. The Australian section of the crowd cheered wildly. Weary proved to us over and over he was a hero by the way he cared for us, but from that moment onwards he was also a football hero. Slim had no idea of the rules of the game but he got the basics at that point: 'You just have to put the ball down over the other team's line!'

Japan's Victory Day was celebrated every month. On 8 December 1942 the kitchens got extra rations and all the guards got drunk. Slim was not real keen to celebrate the bombing of Pearl Harbor with them, so instead he stole a pair of boots from a Jap who'd passed out from too much alcohol and gave them to me. They fitted a bit snugly and could not replace the ones I'd left on the *Perth* so I kept my sandals. In late 1942 it was still easy to slip outside the camp at night and Slim bought supplies from a Chinese man who sold eggs, cigarettes and sweets. We took the sweets to Jimmy in hospital and filled him in on the rugby game. Our visit cheered him up no end but he looked awful. He'd lost weight, his hair was stringy and his bright blue eyes had turned dull.

Some of Slim's *Houston* mates had been on work detail clearing rubble from a bombed warehouse and discovered a stockpile of goodies destined for some faraway village. They found batteries, cooking oil, cigarettes, soap, clothes and tinned food, and smuggled as much as they could back into camp. We knew it would be hard to keep this quiet and someone among the POWs, for God only knew what reason, informed the Japs. When they found out about the batteries the *Kempeitai*, the Japanese secret police, searched the barracks for a week until they found two radios. Their owners were taken away and never seen again and others were bashed for sharing their barracks. We heard a buzz that they were tied to stakes in the ground and beaten, and after they were dead the Japs kept beating them. These and other atrocities were recorded by designated officers, who named the Jap officers for retribution at war's end.

At night the camp came alive with food and other stalls, and for any silver coin you could have whatever you wanted, including a cut or a shave at the barber shop; even the Jap soldiers used it. Every night one bloke stood on a box reading a Charles Dickens book aloud to no one in particular, the same book night after night; he was either off his head or acting, I was never quite sure. He became an attraction for the Japs who rotated their fingers beside their heads and laughed at him like schoolboys, but he had the last laugh. I found out later there was a radio hidden in his box and he would read the book until the Japs weren't around and then quietly give the troops the latest news.

I ran into Lucky Lasslett, who was still acting like the camp electrician until an AIF officer questioned him about it. Lucky told him the story, thinking he would laugh. Wrong; Lucky was demoted to being a normal POW with no perks, tool belt or bandana.

At Christmas, our first in captivity, we erected a palm tree in our mess hall and decorated it with little things the POWs made from whatever they could find or scrounge. The sight of that tree made some men sad, missing their wives and children at home. We all attended the Christmas church services the Japs allowed the chaplain to hold. I heard a story after the war from Chaplain Mathieson about a young Catholic soldier in Changi who was upset he could not attend Christmas Mass. The chaplain made the soldier an honorary Protestant for the day and confirmed it by writing it down on a stamp-sized piece of paper. After the war the chaplain was walking down Elizabeth Street in Melbourne when a young soldier stopped him. Opening his wallet, the soldier pulled out three worn pieces of paper and showed the chaplain the honorary memberships he still carried, one for each Christmas they spent together in Changi as POWs.

Extra rations were bought for Christmas lunch using the camp fund and the cooks did a terrific job, considering our situation. I had lunch with Slim, George, Daniel Baker, Freddie Fuggle and Jimmy, who was finally over his bout of malaria and out of hospital. A tradition in the RAN at Christmas is that the officers serve lunch to the ratings, and we had a hearty beef stew with rice pudding for dessert. Weary Dunlop walked through the mess and asked after our welfare, and he received a hundred back slaps from the men for his match-winning try in the rugby game. Weary was a genuinely likeable bloke, and although we were the Java Rabble and RAN, he considered us his 'crew'.

A few days later we heard that the Java Rabble and other Australian and American POWs were on the go – out of Changi, but to where? No one knew, but I heard a dozen opinions within an hour, as it was all the camp talked about. We didn't have to wait long to find out. In January it was announced that the Japs wanted men to go to Burma and Siam (Thailand). We knew nothing of their plans and had no idea what it all meant, but we heard that there was a long discussion among the Australian command as to who they would send. Black Jack took the decision that 1600 of all the odds and sods should go, including the Dutch, Yanks and the Java Rabble, consisting mainly of *Perth* survivors and all of Weary Dunlop's crew. I learned later that Black Jack's thinking was fairly straightforward: soon the British would retake Singapore and he would then have a division of fit Australian soldiers ready to be rearmed and join the fight against the Japs. I suppose that was strategically sound in theory, but Black Jack and his command sat comfortably in Changi for another three years until war's end, while the numbers of POWs about him shrank.

We had not been told the particulars of who would be moving or where, and in the interim inevitable buzzes started up. They ranged from the most hopeful, a prisoner exchange (which a lot of men believed, especially the married ones, and it contributed to their plunging morale later on), to rumours that we were going to Japan or China, or back to Java or Burma or Siam. It would have been better for everyone if the Japanese had informed us because some men coped badly with the uncertainty, experiencing opposing forces of hope and despair in daily conflict.

Fortunately, in Changi we were responsible for looking after ourselves and mostly left alone by the guards to make do with what we had or could scrounge, and the cooks did the best they could to keep us happy. Changi wasn't too bad but

Jimmy went back into the camp hospital with his second bout of malaria in a couple of months and I worried about him. I knew malaria stayed with you, and all around us blokes were dying of the resulting dehydration.

Early in 1943 we were mustered for cholera shots and told we would be moving out to 'work for the Emperor'. After the needle we were subjected to the most humiliating thing I've ever had done to me: we were made to drop our shorts and bend over while a Jap doctor stuck a glass rod up our bums to check if we already had cholera. To this day I don't know if it is a recognised medical procedure, but none of us had it, apparently.

The whole of the Java Rabble – Australian, American and a lot of Dutch – were to go, over 600 of us. We were also told that an advance party had already been sent. While we didn't know why we were going or exactly where, the buzz was we would be building airstrips for the Japs in their push towards India. Preparations were being made for the journey when something happened that made us wonder whose side our high command was on. As a non-combat officer Weary Dunlop was out of the loop. He knew that the Australian 8th Division had been captured with a warehouse full of medical supplies and he asked if he could take some with us. Changi high command – Galleghan and other officers – had found out we had over 2000 Dutch guilders in our camp fund and told Weary that if he wanted any supplies he had to pay for them. We couldn't believe it. Without Weary and his medical staff many men at the camp would have died. A chief petty officer walked around the camp with a collection box and men donated what little they had to buy the supplies. Some of the officers scheduled to go also donated but did it grudgingly. We managed to smuggle some hospital equipment out of Changi and took everything else not nailed down.

I was assigned to pick up the supplies we'd bought and Slim came with me to lend a hand. Once in stores we nicked a couple of extra boxes of dressings and quinine that we decided could be useful, and no sooner were we out the door than we were stopped by Sergeant Downer, who accused us of stealing. He spoke in a very posh voice, more Pommy than Australian. That accusation bristled; we had no idea where we were going but we well remembered what Java was like, and as far as we were concerned, anything that might ease men's suffering was fair game. Slim would not have a bar of it. He shouted at Downer and called him an 'asshole'. I'd never heard anyone talk to a senior rating like that but Slim wasn't finished, he went off again. 'I saw you with the senior officers at the football game. You think you're one of them.'

The sergeant couldn't be persuaded to change his mind. The two extra boxes were returned to stores and I don't know how many lives could have been saved by them. Sergeant Downer told Slim he'd report him. Slim just laughed in his face and that upset Sergeant Downer even more. It was probably the first time in his life anyone had ever spoken to him like that.

Jimmy turned up just in time to join us. He told us he'd begged the doctors to let him out of hospital. That night I said my goodbyes to Daniel Baker and Freddie Fuggle and asked Daniel to see my parents in Byron Bay when he got home and tell them how much I loved them. It was a sad occasion.

Next morning our Korean guards turned up to our quarters shouting, '*Speedo, speedo*, all men out.' We were only allowed to take what few clothes we had, our dixies and personal items. We mustered outside for the inevitable *tenko*, completed in a record first time. The Korean guards were in a filthy mood, and when we were slow in boarding the trucks the rifle butts came into action again. We four stuck together as we were herded into the truck and packed in like sardines. Speculation was again rife as to our destination. It was all the same to me; just another camp somewhere, we would see. Slim pulled out bottles of quinine and passed them around. He had a medic buddy who said they had plenty and we would probably need it, because odds on there would be hungry mosquitoes wherever we were going.

'Were you reported by Sergeant Downer?' I asked.

'Yes, he wasn't too happy about how I spoke to him. Apparently his father was premier of one of your states. My senior officer told me not to get caught next time and I told him there wouldn't be a next time, because I doubted that Sergeant

Downer was going wherever we were – he's too important for that and will probably stay in Changi until war's end.'

Before we left Changi we'd heard via the hidden radios that Australia was definitely safe from invasion, and that little bit of news cheered us no end. We expected to go to the wharves but the trucks drove away from the harbour and pulled up outside the railway station. We unloaded from the trucks and after another *tenko* men started talking, wondering what type of carriages we'd be travelling in. Anything would have to be better than the rusting hulks we had been crammed into so far.

A Jap officer in charge of the Korean guards allowed us to wander around and buy food from the stalls. Some of the stallholders whispered to us, 'Jap no good. We love Ned Kelly.' It made us feel good. Slim asked who Ned Kelly was and George told him the story.

Slim said, 'Just like our Jesse James.'

'Who's Jesse James?' asked Jimmy.

'Shut up, you silly bugger,' said George.

The Korean guards bunched at either end of the station and sulked because the Jap officer let us wander freely and the Koreans lost face. We would pay for it later.

Chapter 7

Another *tenko* then we were loaded onto the train. Half the carriages were steel boxes that got hot as hell during the day and the other half were timber-sided cattle trucks that got cold at night. With no choice in the matter Slim, George, Jimmy and I got prodded into a cattle truck. We had nothing to keep us warm in the evenings and snuggled up to one another to sleep. We still had no idea where we were going or how long the trip would last; of course, a few blokes kept a book on the 'where' and 'how long'. Once underway, whenever the train stopped to take on water, the Koreans allowed us off to buy whatever food we wanted from the stalls at every station. They were very hard to work out but at last we got their number: they weren't silly – instead of feeding us, they sold our food.

At the end of the first full day we still had no idea where we were headed, but as we travelled north through Malaya we passed thriving towns and villages, rubber, pawpaw and mango plantations, and dense rainforests that reminded me of the ranges around the Tweed Valley. When we moved on to the lowlands we saw farmers ploughing muddy fields behind water buffalo and women following them planting rice. None bothered to look when we waved; work was their life. A couple of RAAF blokes thought we might be going through Siam to Saigon where we could be loaded onto ships to Japan. I never liked that option. We stopped at the Siam border and the Koreans ordered us out, '*Speedo, speedo!*' Dogface, always a particularly cruel bastard, knocked one POW out cold and kicked him as he lay unconscious. He said something in Korean that the other guards found funny. I can tell you, after what we had been through, except for their rifles and bayonets we would have delighted in bashing the lot of them.

We changed trains there and learned we were going to Burma and not to Saigon, which cheered us up; anything was better than going to Japan. We were moved into steel boxcars and fretted about baking in the heat, but luckily it rained all the next day and stayed fairly cool; that improved our mood. We sang songs from home until our throats were raw. The only drawback with travel in the steel boxcars was defecating out an open door while trundling along at 30 miles an hour; we had to depend on our mates to hold us while we did the business.

After the second day we stopped at a station near a port on a wide brown river and the Korean guards were replaced by Japanese soldiers who allowed us off to buy food. We were then loaded onto barges and taken out to the rust-bucket freighter *Moji Maru*, waiting at anchor.

The Japanese crew lined the rail as we climbed aboard. We must have been the first POWs they'd seen and one called out in English, 'Hello, Aussies!'

'Up your arse,' I heard from our ranks.

We climbed down ladders into another stinking cargo hold and sat there for two days, our only chance for fresh air was when we went to use the *benjo*. At our officers' insistence the crew hosed down the top decks to cool them, otherwise we might have died below. Eventually we heard the boilers making steam and then the whining capstan hauling anchor. One of the men using the *benjo* told us he saw our Korean guards coming aboard and that was a bad sign. We sailed in convoy with another rusty transport and a navy escort. Once underway the *Moji Maru* crew erected wind scoops to direct fresh air into the hold, a great relief, but the food was as bad as the cinema. It was at that point that I fully realised how good we'd had it in Changi and longed to go back.

We sailed in flat seas and perfect calm weather, which meant our army mates didn't suffer from seasickness, a great relief in that cramped and dark hold. We'd been given hardtack biscuits by the AIF cooks in Changi to eat with our rice, and that little act of kindness was the last we'd experience for a year.

Next day, while singing to relieve boredom, we heard a low-flying aeroplane above. The hold went quiet as we tried to work out if it was Japanese or not. Then someone looking

Fire breaks out on the freighter Moji Maru

through the hatch identified it as a US fighter bomber. We cheered as one when it flew directly overhead, but when bombs began falling on either side of the ship we knew we were in real trouble. One bomb fell so close alongside that the ship rolled violently, and the helmsman put it over hard to port then starboard to evade the next bomb. The bomber buzzed us once again quite low but dropped no more bombs and then disappeared. The guards threw open the hatch covers and yelled for us to get on deck. We shot up the ladder like rats up a drainpipe and saw that the anti-aircraft gun and crew had been wiped out and a fire had broken out forward close to the ready-use ammunition locker. If that went up we were done for.

There was no shortage of labour – you would call it self-preservation – and we quickly organised a bucket brigade. Some men found undamaged fire hoses and got to work to bring the fire under control. Others helped the crew remove the three dead gun crew; we also managed to relieve them of boots and whatever else they had in their pockets. We reckoned they had blown themselves up with a defective shell because there was no bomb damage but the anti-aircraft gun pit was destroyed. The other transport sailing with us received two direct hits and later we learned that 600 Japanese soldiers and Dutch POWs drowned.

The Japanese naval escort scarpered and left us to pick up the survivors. The Jap skipper was grateful and that night doled out fish soup with our rice and allowed us to remain on the upper deck all night. I remember lying down sleeping and dreaming in the cooling breeze. I was back in my home town of Byron Bay when I was jolted from these pleasant memories by the sounds of low-flying aeroplanes. I quickly jumped to my feet and looked up, expecting more bombs. They were Jap fighter planes. I was so relieved at seeing them and later felt guilty for it.

The next afternoon we arrived at Moulmein, the port for Rangoon, Burma. The town and hills at sunset looked very peaceful. Pagodas covered in gold leaf glistened in the afternoon sun and poked out above the jungle canopy. We decided we wouldn't mind being on work parties there.

Next morning the Korean guards, brutal as always, marched us down the gangway onto the dock for *tenko* and on through town. No one called out to us or tossed food. The people looked fearful, their eyes showing total submission, and I reckoned it had nothing to do with us but with the Japanese. They scurried away from us as we entered the town jail, where we took a decent shower. Apart from the shower there was nothing else good about the place. Our meals consisted of rice with a splash of salty fish sauce. The mossies constantly attacked us at night, and without nets every one of us suffered. I had a cotton sheet for a blanket but they managed to suck my blood through it and we soon used up our supply of quinine pills. The places the Japs picked to hold us always seemed to be rife with malaria and it claimed many casualties amongst the POWs in that jail. After five days of feeding the mossies, over 500 of us were taken outside the jail to stand in formation under a burning sun while a short, fat Japanese officer addressed us. He said we were about to create history by being part of the construction of a railway line from Burma to Siam. He made a point of telling us that the British had been there for over 150 years and had never attempted to build one.

'We,' he shouted, 'the Imperial Japanese Army, intend to make this a gift to the Burmese and Siamese peoples from His Imperial Highness the Emperor of Japan. There will be pay and plenty of food. One day you will proudly tell your families how you were part of the building of this railway line. But if you do not work hard you get no food and there will be no escaping.' He was certainly right about the escaping bit.

We marched out of Moulmein, which was not very big, and the further out of town we got the happier the Burmese people appeared and acted. They threw us rice cakes, cigarettes and fruit, real treats after the jail food, which was the bottom of the barrel – worse than the cinema, and that's saying something. We marched for about twenty minutes to a railway siding where we boarded a train, and a few hours later arrived at Thanbyuzayat, the main administration centre for POWs in Burma and the starting point of the railway line. It also held a couple of thousand men who'd been captured when Rangoon fell. They were mainly British, mates from the Java Rabble and officers who had left Changi before us. We never knew where they had gone till now.

At Thanbyuzayat Australian and British camp staff recorded our names, service numbers, units and ships. Some of our shipmates from the *Perth* had come with an advance party from Changi and set up a canteen in the hospital where we found a few little luxuries. We heard about conditions further up the line and wanted to fatten ourselves up a bit. Slim had kept our winnings from the Crown and Anchor caper for an emergency, and this was just such an occasion. We decided that Jimmy should get Knocka's share and he cried when I told him.

The camp was surrounded by barbed-wire fences. Our Korean guards had left us again, replaced by regular Japanese soldiers. Some were not too bad and at times quite funny in their own way. One day a guard we called Gorgeous George caught one of our blokes talking through the barbed-wire fence to an English-speaking Burmese who was walking a water buffalo. Gorgeous George asked the POW if he was talking and he said no. So the guard asked the Burmese if he was talking. He said no. Then the guard said, 'Someone must get *slappie slappie*,' so he slapped the water buffalo. We all had a good laugh.

Our *Perth* mates were quick to point out ways to survive. At that stage Burmese traders had ready access to the camp and we could buy eggs, palm sugar and sometimes fruit and vegetables. The Jap guards always taxed the Burmese on their way out of the camp. At the start we paid with Japanese occupation script but as the war worsened for the Japs the Burmese only accepted Allied money; no matter what country, money was money, but not script.

Next morning the Java Rabble was loaded into trucks and we didn't see Slim again for three months. We watched him walking away with a couple of American officers, while we sat in the trucks waiting for drivers.

All senior officers, anyone above sublieutenant, remained at the main camp. Our divisional officer was Sublieutenant Taylor, a reserve Kiwi officer from a minesweeper which was captured in Singapore drydock. Taylor was a good bloke and he put his life on the line for his men over the next fifteen months. The Java Rabble stuck together on the fleet of trucks that drove off to Twelve Mile Camp. We were told twice that there were no fences there, once by the Japs and once by our blokes who had been up the track already. We had a natural fence surrounding us, an impenetrable jungle full of poisonous snakes and roaming tigers, and soon we would encounter both, eating the snakes we caught and trying to avoid getting eaten by the tigers.

On arrival we formed up for *tenko* and then the guards turned us over to the AIF colonel in charge of Twelve Mile Camp who assembled us for presentation. The Japanese commandant, who addressed us surrounded by the Korean guards, repeated what we'd been told back at main camp: we were specially chosen to be part of this glorious feat of Japanese engineering, albeit using slave labour. We were not to know just how many chosen ones there would be, but many thousands as I recall.

We were assigned to work on mainly flat land, but the poor buggers working from the Siam side had to contend with mountains, which in the wet season meant flooding rivers and perpetual dampness in steep-sided mountain gorges. In that sense we were on the lucky side, although luck is relative. Our living quarters were basic bamboo lean-to affairs, not a nail or screw to be seen and easily dismantled and moved when necessary. We slept on bunks made of bamboo slats raised about two feet above the ground. Later I found out why. There are only two seasons in the Burmese jungle, dry and wet. The first night of the wet season arrived with a sudden, soaking rainstorm, a welcome relief after the near 100 per cent humidity, and it put us all in good spirits. But that night I thought I'd freeze with only one thin cotton blanket, so I wore my two shirts to bed.

Early in the morning our cooks got working in the kitchens and did their best with not very much. Sublieutenant Taylor told us the routine. 'Okay, men, fill your dixie with rice and bring water to last you all day. There are 30 of us and fifteen picks and fifteen shovels, so you choose and be back here in 30 minutes.'

I chose a pick and half an hour later stood before a Jap Army engineer and two Jap guards. With Sublieutenant Taylor and his shovel we marched about three miles 'up the line', as we called it. Each group was assigned their own section and our supervising officer ensured we did good work. Most of us had boots, shorts and shirts and wore our G-strings as a turban to collect the incessant sweat pouring off our faces. Our job was shoring up embankments, and Sublieutenant Taylor worked alongside us doing the same work we did. After fattening up a bit in Changi we were in pretty good nick, and on that first day we finished early; it was pretty easy for us in the beginning.

The guards allowed us to forage in the forest for anything edible and we found lots of vines covered in berries but were scared to eat them as we suspected some were poisonous. One POW befriended a Korean guard and gave him some berries, but the guard pocketed them so the POW never knew if they were eaten. The guard wasn't sick the next day so we tried a few; they were bitter but no one got sick. I still gave berries a miss after that.

The Japanese had press-ganged thousands of Burmese men into building the line with promises of good pay and conditions. The freshly dug graves on both sides of the embankments showed us the enormous toll paid by the native Burmese workers. They had no machinery, just hand tools, and how they were able to get the line to the stage they had was damn near miraculous.

At the end of the first day the guards blew the whistle and we lined up for *tenko* before marching back to camp and stacking our picks and shovels in a toolshed. It was dark when we got back and our meal of rice with vegetables and fish sauce even tasted quite good. After dinner the camp doctor reminded us to boil our utensils in water before and after each meal.

The next day I remembered an old saying, 'No good deed goes unpunished', when we found our section of work expanded. That taught us an important lesson: never work as if it was our property, work to the set schedule and never get ahead of what we could reasonably be expected to accomplish in a day. That was not the only lesson we learned over the next fourteen months.

Before we left camp the next morning Colonel Ramsay, who was the highest Allied officer at Twelve Mile Camp, had us all out on parade. He said a few words. 'There are men who are looking for the nightingale's nest and, as it is a very shy bird, they would scare it away from its nest. Is that clear?' Us new arrivals didn't have a clue what he was talking about. 'Now carry on with your duties.'

Later on some of the older hands told us what it was all about. There was a radio in camp and snippets of news were given out. It wasn't good enough for some men, who wanted to hear it for themselves and were looking for the radio. It was a clever way of putting it. The Japs who listened to him speak wouldn't have had a clue what he was talking about.

As we progressed and moved up the line, the trip to and from our camp took a little longer each day. We'd return at night buggered, eat what the cooks prepared and collapse onto our bamboo cots. One night we heard guards shouting, 'All men outside.' Hundreds of us were herded into line and we soon learned why we'd been roused from our cots: someone had set the toolshed alight. The Korean guards wandered among our ranks shouting and bashing us, and getting even angrier when we smiled back. The camp commandant made us stand at attention all night and at daylight we had to grab the remains of our picks and shovels and improvise new bamboo handles. He took the shed burning as a personal affront and put our colonel in a bamboo cage in the sun for two days with just water. We Aussies worked together to get the makeshift tools made and then they marched us up the line to do our day's work. They didn't feed us that morning and we got back to camp around midnight, when they still refused to feed us. Some men were so tired they just collapsed, Jimmy among them.

The next morning guards paraded two severely bashed and barely conscious army blokes. The commandant climbed onto his wobbly box and shouted and ranted about how these two men had deliberately lit the fire to sabotage our efforts in helping them construct a fine monument to the people of Burma and Siam. He huffed and puffed and sprayed spittle. There was dead silence from the troops. The Jap commandant wept; I reckon he might have been drunk. The colonel spent another day in the cage. We never found out how the Japs knew who torched the toolshed, or if the men they grabbed were responsible, but we never saw our two men again and the toolshed was never torched after that.

The commandant had a Korean guard, a devout Christian, who wasn't a bad bloke and always looked after the commandant. One night the commandant must have had bad news from home and he got drunk and swaggered through the camp, a bottle of liquor in one hand and his side-arm in the other, singing a mournful song. Practically the whole camp watched his performance and he suddenly started shooting randomly. His performance nearly turned into a nightmare for me when a bullet whistled above my head, passing harmlessly through the hut. He shot off a few more and when he ran out of bullets he disappeared into his quarters. We learned that the Christian Korean walked all night back to the main camp at Thanbyuzayat, returning the next morning with a Jap officer. We never saw the commandant again.

In the dry season, after working all day we'd light bonfires and all the men in camp would spend a few hours singing. That attracted the Burmese traders who came freely into our camp, but unless we had proper money they wouldn't sell us a bean, and since we hadn't been paid since we got there none of us had a brass razoo. They wanted to sell us berries found in the jungle, and our doctor said they could be a good source of vitamins but we had to be careful. A few men, some Java Rabble, died a horrible and painful death after eating one variety. We knew those blokes and mourned every one of them. Attending officers recorded their particulars and we buried them under a crude bamboo cross. In its way, not having money to pay for the food the Burmese sold probably saved lives.

After three months, when we finished our section of the railway embankment we went back to where we'd started and began spreading the ballast brought up on trucks. We had far less distance to travel every day and returned to camp long before sundown, which raised our spirits a little. But not long after, Jimmy came down with the effects of malaria again and became so ill that the camp doctor ordered him to be sent back to our hospital at the main camp. George and I loaded him on a stretcher and put him on the back of a ballast truck. I told him that he'd do anything for a break and he smiled weakly, saluting us; that was the last time we ever saw Jimmy from the *Wollongbar*.

On our way to go up the line the new camp commandant and another Jap officer made us line up and they walked past, inspecting us carefully. The officer pointed out about 30 men, including me, and marched us away to the guards' mess hall, issuing each man new Australian uniform shorts and shirts. Once we were kitted out the Jap guards marched us to a mess-hall set where a Japanese propaganda film crew had laid out bowls of fruit, cigarettes and bottles of cordial and invited us to dig in. We supposed it was intended to show the world how well they treated their POWs. There was not much choice, so we made the best of it and made sure we nabbed all the props before giving back 'our' uniforms and returning to the line. Shovelling ballast was not the hardest work and our section of the track was soon ready for the sleepers and rails.

We lost men regularly to dysentery and malaria, and the beginning of the wet season meant everything went mouldy and anything made of leather or cotton disintegrated. An army bloke in camp specialised in making sandals from worn-out truck tyres and measured me up for a pair after my Japanese boots rotted and split. The jungle heat and high humidity, our greatest enemies, were made worse by the incessant fourteen-to-sixteen-hour work days on reduced rations. Three months of railway work reduced our ranks continually, though lots of replacements arrived and nearly as many died. I couldn't count the dead but I'd say on our side of the railway we lost roughly half our men, both Allied soldiers and Burmese, who had their own section and their own camp.

One night when we got back to camp I got a nice surprise. There in the flesh was Slim, who'd arrived with another batch of POWs: Yanks, Dutch and English. Slim came with them but he was not a part of them. He had a new job, travelling from camp to camp with one Jap guard and paying wages to American POWs in Japanese occupation script. He'd brought a few goodies for George and me: a pawpaw, cigarettes, some Jap script money, two tins of jam and quinine pills. What he told us was the best tonic: Australia and the US were on the counterattack in New Guinea and starting to retake islands throughout western Melanesia, and half the Japanese Pacific fleet had been sunk. I told him about Jimmy and he said he would look him up at main camp.

The wet season dragged on and the whole camp was forced to move to a new camp further up the line. The road was impassable for the trucks due to the monsoon rains so we marched through mud over our ankles for three days to get there. At our new camp we were confronted by a sight I had never seen before. Bearded, unkempt men came out to greet us, gaunt figures with sunken eyes and ribs sticking out who moved one foot to another. Their condition was called 'happy feet', a nasty side effect of beri-beri, a disease caused by vitamin B deficiency and a low-protein diet. Aussies used to high protein were especially susceptible to it. We cried at the sight of them and shared our cigarettes or whatever we had. Some were part of the Java Rabble and, to our shame, we hardly recognised them. Most were sent back to hospital at the main camp but I don't know how many, if any, made it.

The new camp up the line, Camp Number Two, looked better than our old one, but looks were deceiving; the further up the line we went the less food arrived because of pilfering along the way. The commandant made the usual speeches but the tone had changed; we were still expected to build the great railway, but anyone too ill to work got no food. A simple and deadly equation: the Japs wanted the line built but on starvation rations and without proper medical attention. We resorted to foraging and hunting. An old Chinese saying is 'If the back points to the sun you can eat the animal', and since there was not much in the way of rations, when we caught anything, including snakes or birds, we gave them to our cooks who did their best to make it palatable and keep us alive.

Our job was shovelling the ballast trucked up in the dry season, but without the aid of the wooden barrows we'd had at our last camp. Instead we shifted loads of ballast in woven bamboo baskets suspended on bamboo poles. The poles cut into our bony shoulders and we developed ulcers and horrible open wounds. We wondered if we wouldn't prefer to swap jobs with the Dutch, American and British POWs, who were cutting down trees in the forest and making sleepers in readiness for the rails to be brought up in the coming dry season.

The wet season was my worst time as a POW. Water flowed under our cots and every morning we jumped into ankle-deep muddy water and struggled out to the latrine while trying not to slip over in the mud, then dressed in the remnants of our wet clothes, if we had any. Clothes rotted off our backs in the damp conditions, and eventually most of us reverted to the G-string and tyre sandals. We'd go to the kitchen, fill our dixies with rice and make ready for the long march up the line for another twelve-hour shift. We were perpetually hungry and craving things we could never get. Each nation had their own kitchens and we heard the Dutch had good supplies, so one night a few of us paid their kitchen a visit and found an array of tinned foods. We took as much as we could carry, which was plenty as it turned out. The Dutch posted guards at night after that. The Dutch never maintained our hygiene standards so their dysentery cases numbered twenty to our one and they buried their dead daily.

Tropical ulcers became a big problem in the absence of bandages or medical supplies. We tried to scrape the pus and dead skin away with splinters of bamboo. Men had cricket-ball-sized holes in their legs and the medics often had to go in as far as the bone and scrape away the dead tissue. Done after work in our barracks, it was known as 'crying time'. The worst of the infections caused men to lose the leg below the knee. That was the last thing I wanted because my own father lost a leg in the Great War in France and I knew of the problems he had later in life.

One night we came back from the line, exhausted and in very low spirits, and found Weary Dunlop and some of his medical staff in camp. The medical people used to move up and down the line, and they were sickened at the sight of our condition and set about trying to control our beri-beri with yeast tablets and by introducing more of the local sugar into our diet. Men with extreme cases of beri-beri got duck eggs when available and the best care Weary could give them. The work and nonstop rain eventually got to us all. Men dropped daily and it was all we could do to carry them back to camp at night. I learned to get to the front of the work parties going out and coming back because the guards used bayonets on any stragglers, although we kept the pace as slow as we could.

As careful as I was, I knew I was getting very sick and one morning awoke feeling worse than usual, sweating and shivering. It became apparent to Sublieutenant Taylor that I was in a bad way and he argued with the guards, who eventually allowed me to report to sick bay. 'Sick bay' was the name we gave to the big log we sat on while waiting for attention. George said whatever I had I'd beat, but I didn't like the look in his eyes. I thought that was it, that I'd lie down and never get up as so many of my mates had done. I got in line at the sick bay and sat on the log. Later I felt a hand on my shoulder and looked up; it was Weary Dunlop himself.

'You're the baby of *Perth*, aren't you?' I nodded and attempted to stand. He put a hand on my shoulder. 'No, stay there. We'll have you right, son.'

'Yes, sir,' I said.

He spoke to an orderly who led me to a 'bed' where I was given quinine tablets and covered with a blanket. The first few days of delirium were the worst. Weary argued daily with the Jap commandant who thought I was malingering, but Weary

Treatment in the sick bay

won the argument and I rested under his care. I woke up one evening to find George waving a fan made from palm leaves over me. I asked him how long he had been there.

'Long enough to hear all about your parents and friends in Byron Bay, but you didn't make much sense. You can tell me all about it when you get better.'

'It's a promise, if I get out.'

'You'll get out alright. An orderly said you're getting better every day. I should have a nice surprise for you tomorrow.' I hated surprises. I'd had enough from our captors.

'Do you want to know what it is?'

I nodded.

'We have an Aborigine from the 8th Divvy with us and we're going fishing in the stream we cross up the line. This bloke showed us how to make a trap using rocks; it takes no time to build and we should find out tomorrow if we were successful. We made a deal with the Japs, who love fish, and we're going fifty-fifty with any we trap. I'll see you soon, Stoker, with some fresh fish.'

I saw George again a couple of nights later. 'It worked. The Japs took half the fish and we gave the rest to the hospital kitchen.'

True to his word, my next meal was soup with chunks of fresh fish, rice and something green, all very good for the patients and our morale. We thanked George and the fishermen by getting better.

I watched Weary Dunlop in action; he never stopped and he looked after much more than the sick bay. He lectured the men on the necessity of hygiene in camp and insisted everyone clean all utensils in nothing less than boiling water. He organised some men to dig properly covered latrine pits, and his attention to the basics helped save many lives. He improvised using bamboo intravenous needles and treated us better than anyone had in my time in Burma. His concern for our health boosted camp morale daily.

On his morning rounds Weary came in and looked me over. I told him I thought I was ready to go back on the line. He told me not to be so keen and made me stay on my back for two more days. As soon as he thought I was right he tipped me a wink and I went back up the line.

We often worked eighteen-hour days and gradually moved further away from camp as the line slowly progressed, and then marched up to four miles back. We'd have a couple of hours' sleep then go back to work again. We reckoned the theory was to work us to death and replace us with other POWs. We were sure it wouldn't be long before we were moved to a new camp further up the line, and one day at *tenko* we got the word: 'Everybody move.' It was back to our barracks, grab our meagre possessions and march through the mud to the next peg further up. Our numbers dwindled daily and our officers kept a record of the dead and their death date. Most of our bodies were broken but, and this is only one man's opinion, I think men began dying from a broken heart. On the long march to our new camp our Japanese guards forced us onwards mercilessly, and we didn't bury any men who died along the way; the Japs forbade it. We couldn't stop, so we closed their dead and unseeing eyes, arranged the bodies with as much dignity as we could, covered them with branches and left them alone in the jungle to the wild animals. I admit we had little sentiment left in us, but I knew those men and I can never forget leaving our fellow Australians like that.

After three days we arrived at our new camp, which we called Camp Number Three, and found Dogface, the Brown Bomber and the rest of the hated Korean guards there. We hoped we had lost them. Here, so far from civilisation, they became even more vicious and took to bashing us for trivialities. To make matters worse they appeared to have an endless supply of alcohol, and when they drank they became truly unhinged. One night the obviously drunk camp commandant spotted one of our blokes coming back from the latrine and, for reasons I will never understand, shot him dead. The Korean guards laughed at the poor chap in his G-string, even the commandant joined in. They would not let us near him until the morning when we buried him. I hoped our officers recorded that crime and reported it at war's end, and that the bastard responsible took 'the long drop'.

One particular night it rained by the bucket on our way up the line. Just when we thought we couldn't be shocked by anything, we saw decomposing bodies floating up and out of their shallow graves, mainly natives, but men nonetheless. On the line the guards constantly beat us and shouted, '*Speedo, speedo.*' We couldn't have worked any faster even if we wanted to; we were the walking dead, weak beyond words and, but for our spirits, broken. The food and conditions encountered at that camp were by far the worst, and the many men with dysentery made it uncomfortable for everyone. At night, with few other distractions, we picked lice and bugs off each other. The other diversion was telling stories about our homes. One night it was my turn and I talked about the Northern Rivers region of New South Wales.

My dad and his four brothers were born and raised in Byron Bay and went off to the Great War, the one we heard would end all wars. On returning from the madness of the front in France and Belgium, they all took up soldier settlement blocks at Dunoon, a little village outside of Lismore, where I was born. As my father had lost a leg in the war he found the clearing and ploughing of farm life too difficult, so he moved the family back to Byron Bay and sold his block to his younger brothers. After settling in Byron Bay he bought a hansom cab, then upgraded to a motor taxi in the mid-1930s, which made life easier.

I went to primary school in Byron then to high school in Mullumbimby, where I met Daniel Baker. I travelled to and from school by train, sometimes having to wait until the banana train went past before my train could leave, and meaning I didn't get home until after dark. (The banana train always had right of way so the fruit cargo could be loaded onto ships and travel south.) We knew about the Depression but it did not affect us, as there was plenty of work for any who wanted it. We were surrounded by many dairy farms that supplied Norco, the largest dairy cooperative in the southern hemisphere. They made cheese, ice-cream and butter, all of which they shipped south on the SS *Wollongbar*. In those days in Byron Bay, we also had an abattoir and the dressed meat went out on the *Wollongbar* as well. Andersen's Piggery was the local maker of a large variety of smallgoods and provided work for many of the townsfolk, including me, after school. They shipped their goods by train and ship, and I always looked forward to seeing Jimmy when I delivered smallgoods to the *Wollongbar* on the long pier that stretched 600 yards out into Byron Bay. I had another part-time job at the pub, doing odd jobs that included running bets for the SP bookie. In those days we also had a thriving timber industry, but eventually all the native stands disappeared into sawmills to make way for the growing dairy farms. Every month the bishop of Grafton came to Byron Bay and said a special Mass. He often went on about the evils of alcohol, but it never stopped him accepting the free bottle of Scotch whisky the publican had me deliver to the presbytery. I was given a shilling for my trouble.

Not long after the shooting incident we got a new camp commandant whose role was to bring some sort of organisation to the camps he visited. We never knew if the old commandant was moved because he shot and killed an RAN sailor or if it was normal rotation, but we were glad of it because dealing with the Korean guards was hard enough. We knew who were the nasty ones and who were the ones we could corrupt; that knowledge was important and helped us survive. The new commandant made Weary Dunlop assemble his crew and medical team and congratulated us for the progress we'd made.

Out of the blue Slim turned up again. This camp was the same as the others, with a mix of American, Dutch, British and Aussie POWs, so he had the Yanks' pay. We told him we had not been paid for a long time and he said that Rohan Rivett, the journalist we were with from Java, would be here any time soon.

'Yeah, as soon as the wet season is over,' said George, who had never liked Rivett.

Slim had some goodies for us: about a pound of tobacco and a bottle of vitamin pills. Slim asked me if I could take him to Weary Dunlop's tent; it seemed a little strange, but who was I to question our guardian angel. Slim carried a haversack and asked me to stay outside and let him know if anyone was coming. I nodded my head; I was just a simple stoker. When he was finished I asked no questions and led him back to our barracks. We sat around while Slim told us news of the war. He said that the USA, the biggest industrialised nation in the world, was in full war production, with planes, ships and tanks being produced in record numbers. Germany was constantly being bombed. The Japs were being pushed back. Japanese shipping was being sunk in record numbers by submarines, depriving their factories of necessary war materials. That was why they wanted the railway line finished, we supposed. At least now we knew for sure that home was safe, which pleased us no end.

Slim left again. George and I had a plan. We had tobacco but no paper. One of our blokes had a Bible. We tore pages out and the three of us rolled up cigarettes then took them down to the Dutch camp, where we swapped them for tinned condensed milk and other food. We split the trade three ways.

There was to be more good news for us the next day. At *tenko* we were told that all men could scribble a couple of lines on a letter card that would be sent to our next of kin. We had to wait in line to use the few pencils there were and wondered if it was a trick. It wasn't; it took a while but my family did receive it.

The lie of the land was starting to flatten out to rice paddy fields away from the jungle, and in the distance we could make out mountain ranges.

George said, 'I hope we finish before we have to tackle that.' I agreed with him.

We were now laying the sleepers. George and I worked as a team carrying them, as most men did. We couldn't help but notice the farmers in the distance working their fields with water buffalo. George and I looked at one another and smiled. That night we sat down with Sublieutenant Taylor to present a plan that needed a lot of POWs to be involved in if it was to be successful. We knew he was on friendly terms with Kim, the Christian Korean guard, and that a lot of the guards were doing it much tougher than the Japanese, though not as tough as us. It took a few days to organise everyone. A knife was found for one of our army blokes, who was a butcher. The cooks organised their pots and fires. We had a burial party briefed to disappear the skin, horns and bones before the farmer and commandant came looking for the beast in the morning. All the Koreans wanted was the offal, which suited us just fine.

On the chosen day there was plenty of cloud cover and the night was black. We crept out and knew the general direction of where the farmers were, stopping sometimes to listen for the water buffalo's bells. The farmers never kept them close to their house, for whatever reason, which decreased our chances of getting caught. We finally found it, undid its tether and removed the dinger from the bell. On the three-mile trip back to camp it started to rain heavily, and for once that was a blessing as it washed away any tracks. I tripped and fell on some logs, the pain searing straight to my brain; I had opened up my now healing ulcers, the mud oozing into them. I knew I was in for more pain.

We snuck back into camp where everyone was waiting. The butcher quickly dispatched the beast then the skin and bones were buried with the bell, the cooks had the meat in the pots and Sublieutenant Taylor delivered the offal to the Koreans. At sun-up the farmer arrived and, with the camp commandant, held a tour of the camp; the cooks all smiled at one another as they tended their fires; it sure was a mystery how a beast could possibly disappear without a trace.

George and I did it again about a month later further up the line. We did feel a little guilty about taking the locals' means of labour, but with a diet of mainly rice it was a matter of survival; we had no choice. The Dutch side of the camp heard about our little party trick and decided they would pull the same stunt. The secret to our success was not to do it so often. It cost them four dead and no water buffalo to work that out.

Some of our doctors used to play chess at night with our new camp commandant and help drink his whisky, of which he had ample supplies. So when the Jap engineers went back to base camp for a meeting, the docs convinced the commandant to declare a *yasume*, a day of rest or a holiday. It was most welcome, as we all needed it. My tropical ulcers were now very bad; no amount of scraping would stop the pus. At the sick bay the orderly called Weary over.

'You should have come earlier,' he said, smiling as he prodded the gaping hole. 'I have no drugs left to treat you, son. I'll tell you what I am going to do. You are going back to base camp hospital.'

'Sir, I don't want to leave my mates.'

He sat back on his stool and sighed. 'Son, if you don't go back I am going to chop your leg off.'

'I'll go, sir,' I replied hastily.

I said my goodbyes to George and the rest of the blokes. 'George, don't forget to ring my parents.'

'You're a silly bugger,' he replied, 'you'll be back. We're not going to get rid of you that easy.'

Chapter 8

There were about twenty of us walking wounded and we had one guard with us. Trucks were still unable to use the road, so through the mud we slogged, taking two days to cover the 30 miles that the line now stretched over. Along the way we passed a section of Jap soldiers dragging and pushing field guns; they never asked nor did we offer our help. They joked with our guard; we guessed they were in no hurry to reach the Burma front line. We arrived at a clearing where a hissing steam engine stood, towing six uncovered wagons. Boxes of stores were unloaded and bags of rice readied to be moved up the line. It looked to us that the wet season was coming to an end with the clear blue skies, and I felt happy for my mates left up the track. But looks can be deceiving – it was to be a long wet season.

The train was a luxury for us as we cruised back to Thanbyuzayat, the main POW base camp. We passed our old camps and waved at slouch-hatted, G-string-wearing diggers doing their bit on the line. Passing the camps I noticed the cemeteries were twice as big, just like my leg. From boarding the train to main camp it only took about eight hours, the main worry for us on the journey being a lone American bomber that swooped down so low on the train it nearly burst my eardrums. We waved like hell at him and the plane moved its wings from side to side before disappearing. There was a lot of conjecture among us about his reasons; maybe he had no bombs left or noticed our white skin. That's one I shall never know the answer to.

Things looked pretty rosy at base camp compared to where we had come from. We grabbed our possessions – my cigarette tin, a pair of shorts, shirt, dixie, mug and the G-string I had on – and disembarked, helped by medical orderlies. New arrivals to the camp from Changi just stood and stared. We knew completely how they felt at the sight of us; apart from our rice and biscuits on the first day of the journey we had not eaten in 24 hours. Our particulars were recorded then we were taken for a meal – poor by conventional standards but much better than we were used to. We went for delousing next, and what clothes we had were removed to be washed. Then we had the luxury of luxuries – a hot shower, the first in four months, using a native soap which smelled terrible but did the job – before we were allowed to go to the hospital. When the doctors admitted us I was told that they didn't scrape ulcers anymore, they just cleaned them and applied special medicine. The cleaning was just as painful as the scraping but only had to be done once, thank God.

There were hardly any navy boys in main camp, mainly diggers from Changi. I had to keep my leg up and was in bed, a luxury I could have only dreamt of up the track. I kept asking army boys if they knew Daniel Baker or Freddie Fuggle. The word must have got around and I had a visitor from the administration office who told me they were up the line. 'I don't know where,' he said. 'Don't worry, mate, I will find them.'

After a couple of weeks my leg was responding to treatment. The doctors said it would take a month.

Obviously there must have been radios in the camp with the amount of news that was buzzing around, all good for our side. Every couple of days US bombers would fly over the camp on missions; either we were not near military targets or they had good intelligence.

One day I heard a Texan voice call, 'Stoker.' I knew who it was immediately and sat up.

I smiled at Slim. 'How did you know?'

'George told me – he said to tell you he's doing fine.'

'The lying bastard,' I said.

Slim brought me fruit, a chocolate bar and a packet of tailor-made French cigarettes. He asked me if I needed anything.

I said, 'No, mate, I'm fine.'

'Here, take this.' He handed me a wad of Burmese rupees. 'You can still buy off the traders with these; they won't take the Jap script anymore.' Slim told me he would be leaving camp tomorrow.

'Where to?' I asked.

'Up over the Thai side of the line, not far from your last camp.'

'What are you doing going that far?'

Slim smiled at me and said, 'I'll tell you some day, if I'm still alive.' Then he said with a wry smile, 'The line is nearly finished.'

He was wrong; there was five months' work still to be completed. There was another buzz that all prisoners at Thanbyuzayat camp were to be sent back to Changi. It was wrong too.

My tropical ulcers were healing slowly; it's marvellous how your body can mend itself with just basic food and medicine. With a pair of bamboo crutches I was able to move around the camp. The army boys made me feel at home, but home to me was up the line with my *Perth* shipmates. Practically every day there was something on in the camp, which in real life was no big deal but to us was heaven-sent, a distraction from the brutal guards and loss of freedom. Home was always on your mind. I still hadn't had a reply from my parents after the Red Cross letter-gram I sent. You just didn't know if the Japs had actually allowed them to be sent; the letters might have been sitting in a warehouse somewhere until the Japs wanted to distribute them, just another form of torture, mental this time, as there were buzzes around the camp saying just such a thing. I had resolved to live one day at a time and not to believe buzzes.

One night there was a picture on, the first I had seen since I was home on Christmas leave in 1941. It was pure Japanese propaganda: footage of the cowardly attack on Pearl Harbor and the Imperial Japanese Army marching into the POW-lined streets of Singapore. The army blokes in the audience would call out some of the faces as the camera panned around. 'Rewind,' they would call out to the Jap operator, all to no avail, as the Jap would look at them and smile as he puffed on a cigarette, thinking they must like the show. They also had footage of their submarines at work; ironic as the Allied submarines were now exacting revenge on their shipping. The voiceover was gloating but I knew the tide of war was changing. I just had to bide my time.

The wet season showed signs of breaking. The sun is a great healer; the orderlies, when they changed my bandages, would tell me to sit out in the morning sun for half an hour before redressing. I didn't need crutches anymore and had been discharged from hospital to a barracks full of Pommies and some Australian soldiers who were mates of Daniel Baker and Freddie Fuggle. I knew Daniel and Freddie were up the line but still didn't know which camp. I was hoping Slim could help me find out but I didn't know when I would see him again.

One night a camp concert was put on. As usual the Jap officers took up the front row and admired the men dressed up as women. One Jap guard was seen peeping into the tent where they were putting on their dresses and makeup.

A couple of the blokes walked up and surprised him. He thought they wanted a look too. They laughed; he just smiled and went back to peeping.

There were a lot of professional musicians, actors and comedians, who the Japs never quite got but they clapped when we cheered. Back in our barracks the Pommy blokes told us about different acts from England who were famous there; some blokes had salacious gossip about some of the men who would dress up as girls. I was glad that I had my mother to think of.

There was a bulletin board in camp and every day I would check it for any news from up the line, remembering there wasn't a lot of pen and paper up there, especially during the wet season. There was a big poster proclaiming a *yasume* day for Thanbyuzayat; we were to have a Melbourne Cup event. Apparently there were a lot of Japs here who'd been at the Changi version and were very keen for us to stage another, and there was a buzz that the top general and his staff were attending. With the re-running of the Cup I realised it must be November 1943 and I had been a POW for 21 months. My urge to survive this muck became even stronger. I just needed a little luck, like I was having now.

There was a specially built viewing platform for the officers, and the Japanese general arrived in a Rolls-Royce with the Rising Sun painted on the doors. All officers and men in the camp were lined up as if on parade. The Jap general walked among the ranks as if he was the governor-general of Australia. We watched in envy as the staff cars were unloaded in front of us, cases of grog and food for their special *yasume* day. They had the pick of the crops.

The Melbourne Cup was run and won. It had all the trappings of our previous one: bookies; men dressed as women, who were starting to look very desirable; and the race caller. I even tried the rice wine the cooks had made to up the excitement but all I got was sick. The cooks had been learning, though; they had discovered how to make flour from the rice, mixing it with palm sugar to make dumplings, which to me was a special treat that I have not encountered since.

More men from Changi began arriving at our camp and were sent up the line. The Japs' urgency to finish the line could be felt in the camp. The wet season should have been over but it was unusually long in 1943. We heard news via the secret camp radios that the Japs were losing a lot of men and supplies to US submarines – supplies which were much needed in their push through Burma to their ultimate goal of India. The Burmese people were starting to form resistance movements in response to the harsh treatment of their people. The Japanese Greater East Asia Co-Prosperity push was all one way, and 'better the white man you know' would no doubt have been their thinking, as every day we heard reports of Burmese men and women being executed.

After two months of rest and recuperation I was informed that I was going back up the track. I quickly bought as many tins of food as I could afford. In the wet season sandals were alright, but I also wanted a pair of boots for the dry season. I heard that the hospital orderlies sold the boots off dead men and used the funds to buy food for the hospital. I got lucky and even got a pair of woollen socks. I was ready for the line.

There were about 100 men who mustered for the *tenko*. I had a sugar bag half full of tinned food along with my pair of shorts and one shirt. Hats were hard to come by so my G-string became my turban once more. Many of the men knew I had not been up the line before and were asking me what it was like. I only had one answer for them: it changes every day. We marched down to the waiting train. I was full of expectations of catching up with my *Perth* mates. I had made a point of not making any close bonds with these new blokes; I had become 'used to' death and watching the suffering of old mates had made me immune from reaching out to new friends.

As the train slowly chugged up the line I marvelled at the amount of work that had been achieved through virgin jungle with just basic tools such as axes, picks and shovels, but the cost had been the enormous suffering and deaths of fellow human beings, both native Burmese and POW slave labourers. You knew we were getting close to camps when we saw men, many wearing slouch hats with tools in hand, with the Jap guards standing back from the line. Some waved, most didn't.

The train stopped at the Twelve Mile Camp I had been in. There were no sweet memories here for me, and no old mates. We were unloaded for a toilet stop then we unloaded the stores for the camp from the train. We had a young Pommy officer with us who was bombarded with questions from his men for which he had no answers. 'How far to the next camp?' they asked. He looked at me.

'It's an overnight trip,' I told him.

We were given our boiled rice and told to reboard the train. A couple of Pommies came over and sat next to me to ask questions, just what I didn't want. I felt I had to tell them something; they wanted to survive.

'Make sure you immerse your dixie and mug in boiling water before and after eating. Don't drink unboiled water. Don't give the guards any excuse to bash you. And last but not least, don't work too hard.'

Later on that trip to the next camp, one of our number, who to this day I believe must not have been right in the head, committed suicide by jumping headfirst off the train into a tree. You could hear his skull pop. The officer and men in our covered wagon said a prayer for him. I thought, you can say all the prayers you like, but no one will help you but yourself.

Next day we arrived at Camp Number Two; I was excited at the thought of catching up with George and the crew. The Korean guards were all new to me, but just as brutal; they rifle-butted anyone too slow to form up for their obligatory *tenko.* As they counted they kept coming up one short, and the Pommy officer tried to explain about the suicide. They just could not understand till the camp commandant arrived. I knew he could speak English.

When he was told the story he just nodded his head, saying, 'Very honourable.'

Yeah, bullshit, I thought.

We marched into the camp and I could see no faces I recognised. I noticed our cemetery had expanded and hoped George wasn't in it. We marched up to my old barracks; it was empty, and I realised they must have moved up the line. That's when I understood the Japs' plan: I would never be catching up with my old mates because, with plenty of POWs, they just kept pushing fresh men into the line to replace the dead or living dead.

I waited for the work parties to come back to camp; it was nearly midnight before they arrived. The slouch-hatted men slowly trudged into camp. They were exhausted and didn't look in good shape. Watching as they got their rice from the cooks, I noticed Daniel Baker and Freddie Fuggle and made my way over to them.

'Stoker!' they cried out together.

We shook hands and I told them I had some goodies I would share with them. I asked if they knew where the *Perth* boys were and they told me they weren't here when they arrived. They also said the Japs were making them work extra hours so the line could join up with the Thai side. The Japs had them light bonfires so they could work at night and had told them that very soon they would be going to a holiday camp.

'Don't believe a word they say, mates,' I said. I had heard it before.

It was still in the extended wet season and the Jap engineers were pushing us harder. I was in fairly good shape now and kept close to Daniel and Freddie, trying to help them with their section of work. With the ground being so wet, any torrential downpours meant the banks we were working on got washed away, so we had to start shovelling the washouts once again. A section that would take six hours to complete in the dry season took double that in the wet. The Jap engineers must have been under a lot of pressure to have their section finished in time for the dry season, as they stayed with us the whole time. The guards with us became more vicious, belting anybody they thought was not working hard enough. I couldn't wait for the dry to start but in fact we still had at least another month of the wet season to go.

Once again, trudging back to camp I always tried to lead the work party, walking just fast enough but not too slow, to keep the blows from the guards to a minimum. We would arrive back in camp at ten or eleven at night, eat our rice and climb onto our bunks, no mattress, just one skinny blanket and bamboo slats. Sleep would come from exhaustion. The attap roof leaked and water would flow under the beds. Life

Some crew members of HMAS *Perth* astride one of the ship's big guns, 1941, the year before the ship was torpedoed.
AWM 006602

Only eighteen and off to sea: Stoker Lloyd Munro.

Captain Hector Macdonald Laws 'Hard Over Hec' Waller, DSO, RAN, smoking a pipe on the bridge of HMAS *Stuart*, the vessel he commanded before the *Perth*. AWM 005002/13

ABOVE: At Camp Bicycle, POWs were reduced to using G-strings like those worn by these men, standing in front of makeshift bamboo urinals. AWM 157869
BELOW: The camp in September 1945, with relieved ex-POWs lounging on the veranda of the sleeping quarters. AWM 123669

ABOVE: A photograph taken by Australian POW, George Aspinall, inside Changi in September 1942, during the stand-off about signing allegiance to the Japanese Empire. AWM P00077.017

BELOW: The theatre at Changi. The productions were enthusiastically appreciated by POWs and their captors. AWM P01433/010

Railway life: jungle camps and hard labour. ABOVE: No 2 Staging Camp in August 1943. AWM 132944 BELOW: Laying pieces of track. AWM P00406.027

Lieutenant Colonel E.E. Dunlop, Commanding Officer 2/2nd Casualty Clearing Station, (right) and Lieutenant Colonel A. E. Coates, Chief Medical Officer, at Nakhon Pathom hospital. AWM 117362

A hospital hut in Thanbyuzayat, Burma. AWM 043270

A view of Tamarkan, Thailand, in September 1945. Stoker hoped his friend George would remain here in relative safety after Stoker left for Japan. The huts with thatched attap roofs and open walls were luxury after what the men had endured on the line. AWM P01910.010

The trip to Phnom Penh was in trucks like these. AWM P00406.010

Stoker must have looked pretty much like these oil-soaked survivors of the *Rakuyo Maru* who were rescued and cleaned up by the USS *Sealion*. All in all 160 POWs were saved by US subs. AWM 305634
AWM 305636

Tamarkan, Thailand. c1944, at the dedication ceremony of the memorial to persons who lost their lives building the Thai–Burma Railway. AWM 118788

A bunch of grateful survivors. These were men – mostly Australian – picked up by the USS *Barb*.
TOP ROW: Jimmy Johnson (Brit), Leo Cornelius, Thomas Carr (Brit), Stoker Lloyd Munro, Al Allbury (Brit), Robert Hampson, Neville Thams, Augustus Fuller (Brit), Jim Campbell.
BOTTOM ROW: Harold New, Muray Thompson, Jack Flynn, Cecil Hutchinson, Ross Smith.

was monotonous, and it was near impossible to keep dry. One morning, after another torrential storm, I passed some new graves on my way to the latrines; they had been washed away and the newly buried corpses were floating. Sometimes there was just not enough energy to bury them as deep as they should go. Food was also a problem again with the wet season. Men were coming down with dysentery and some were developing beri-beri from a lack of vitamins. The army blokes I was now with had come straight from Changi where they'd had clean water, and quite often I would see them drinking unboiled water and not washing their dixies in the boiling water provided. We only had a couple of young Pommy doctors who had no medical supplies or experience.

One morning we lined up for work and Colonel Ramsay told us to go back to our huts and collect our belongings. We were moving camp up the line. He also told us that Weary Dunlop had a new hospital where we were going. With that news even the sick men decided to take a punt and join the not so sick. The trains never went any further than the camp we were in and the tracks that were used in the dry season were impassable so we had to slog it out on foot. The mud was at least a foot deep in places. The sick were by now wishing they had stayed. We lost a few men and the Japs wouldn't allow us to bury them. They were just placed into the jungle. I don't know how far it was but it took us two days of slogging before we arrived, and it was the same camp that I'd been at when

Marching from Changi with belongings in hand

Weary Dunlop treated me for leg ulcers – Camp Number Three. At least they were expecting us and had a hot meal prepared, boiled rice. I asked one of the cooks if there were any *Perth* POWs there. 'Haven't seen any,' he said. I had no fond memories of this place, except for the time we raided the Dutch storeroom, but there was to be no repeat of that. In fact, the Dutch section of the camp was to be moved back to base camp; their numbers had been severely depleted and they were in very poor condition. They were to be replaced by 500 Burmese 'volunteers'. Weary Dunlop and most of his medical team had been moved up the line, much to our detriment.

Working with the army boys was a learning experience, a different way of doing things. We were working longer hours; the guards were constantly shouting '*speedo*' and bashing men they considered too slow. One afternoon one of our blokes snapped and planted his shovel firmly on one guard's face, knocking him out. The other guards came running and grabbed the offender, dragging him into the jungle. We heard him scream then silence. The guards came back laughing, blood still visible on their bayonets.

With the departure of the medical team hygiene standards in the camp had started to drop. It was left to us to try to educate the Burmese in how to do the right thing. It was a pretty hard task to get them to change the way they had done things all their life. It got to the stage where I wouldn't use the camp latrines, preferring to wait till I went up the line and go in the jungle, always looking over my shoulder, as we had seen tigers a few times. I had my shovel with me, just in case.

Daniel Baker and Freddie Fuggle, along with some of their mates, were not travelling very well in these conditions. Not fit enough to go out on the line, they worked in a detail to bury the dead. It was hard enough, but not as long a day as being up the line. With the arrival of the Burmese in our camp the dreaded cholera reared its ugly head. They were upstream from us and used the streams as toilets. I was worried about Daniel and Freddie being so close to it. At least the wet season was over and trucks were able to use the track, bringing up ballast for the line. We knew that as soon as we had it laid out trains would be able to use it and I was hoping that the sick would be able to be transported back to Thanbyuzayat, including Daniel and Freddie. But it was not to be – they both contracted cholera and died within a day of each other. I was not allowed to say my goodbyes to them. The camp doctor decided that cholera victims would no longer be buried; instead they were to be burned. I helped with the funeral fire. A bugler played the last post and their divisional officer had some kind words to say. I picked some flowers from the jungle and tossed them on the fire. No tears were shed, we were just too tired. Christmas was approaching and for me it was not to be a happy one under any conditions. I had lost too many mates.

With the line nearing completion we could see much more activity overhead from the American bombers on their way into Burma, knowing full well that the line would become a strategic target for them. The POW camps straddled the line and the Japs refused to allow us to build bomb shelters. Working on the line one day we heard the clanging of logs being hammered up ahead. We knew the sound; it meant we would soon be joining up with the line from Thailand. We were not to know that a joining of the line ceremony had already been held, a little prematurely I might add, as we still had not finished the ballast at our end. So it was more *speedo*. One time the Japs made us stay up the line for two whole days and nights with no covering and just boiled rice cooked on-site, such was their haste to have the line finished.

The first train that arrived on the joined line from Thanbyuzayat brought us meat and fruit. The fruit was given to the hospital patients, and even though the meat was a bit whiffy we still ate it. One bloke who was sitting next to me all of a sudden started coughing; I thought he was going to vomit. Next minute he stuck his fingers down his throat and started to pull at something. We just watched as he extracted a huge tapeworm out of his mouth; it must have been about ten feet long. That was a first for me.

'No wonder I'm so skinny,' he said.

One wag replied, 'It wouldn't have anything to do with being starved of food, would it?'

The bloke cut the worm up, taking great pleasure in torturing it.

Chapter 9

A large notice had been posted on the bulletin board up the line:

> *A letter of condolence on the occasion of the memorial service for deceased POWs. As the final stage of the railway construction has now been completed I am, on this day of commemoration of consoling the souls of the POWs of the third branch, remembering the 665 who have died in this district during the past year. In my opinion it is a virtue, since ancient times, to pay homage to the souls who have died in war, even though they may be enemies. Moreover you were under my command and have endeavoured to work diligently in obedience to my orders, while always longing for the final repatriation to your own country once the war is over and peace is restored. I have always done my utmost to discharge my duty conscientiously, taking responsibility for all of you as your commander.*
>
> *Now that you have passed onto the other world, owing to the unavoidable prevailing diseases and indiscriminate bombing, I cannot see you in this world anymore. I cannot help shedding tears, sympathising with your unfortunate circumstances. This*

tragedy is the result of war, however. It is owing to fate that you
are in this condition and I consider that God has called you here.
However, today I try to console your souls and pray for you in my
capacity as your commander, together with other members of my
staff, by dedicating a cross and placing a wreath in your cemetery.

In the very near future your comrades will be leaving this
district, consequently it may be impossible to offer prayers
and lay a wreath in your cemetery for some time to come. But
undoubtedly some of your comrades will come here again after
the war to pay sincere homage to your memory.

Please accept my deepest sympathy and regards and may you
sleep peacefully and eternally.

Given on the 20th day of November in the year of Showa.

Yoshitida Nagatomo, Lieutenant Colonel Chief of No. 3
Branch of Thai War Prisoner Camps

It was at least six weeks old. I struggled to figure them out. They beat, starved and killed us, then came and put a piece of wood into the ground with a bunch of flowers and everything was alright. I didn't think so.

There was a large group of men around the noticeboard, some asking, 'What does it all mean? Are we going home?'

'I doubt it. It's not over till it's over.'

I was slowly walking back to my barracks when I heard a God-almighty commotion. I went to have a look. Three men were carrying the largest python I had ever seen, still wriggling, towards the kitchen – fresh meat with our rice tonight.

Next day a *yasume* was proclaimed for us to celebrate the completion of the line. I had a few bob left in my tin and went down to the canteen. I was in luck: the Burmese trader had just been and, looking for a treat, I got a banana, one boiled duck egg and two cigarettes. I just wanted to be by myself so I headed towards the stream that ran through the camp. I sat down under a tree and slowly peeled the egg, seeing how far I could flick each piece of shell into the stream. Watching my pieces float freely away, I slowly devoured the egg then had my banana for sweets. This was the first time I had been able to be truly alone in a long time, and different thoughts were bouncing around in my head. I felt a little guilty about my shipmates up the line. Would I see them again? They had been the one constant for me since becoming a POW; other faces of men who had not made it swiftly went out of focus. My thoughts turned to home, wondering how Mum and Dad were coping. We still hadn't received any mail, though that was much harder for the married men to deal with.

All of a sudden my peace and tranquillity was disturbed by a group of laughing and giggling Burmese coolies who had the biggest cigarette I had ever seen; they seemed to be having a good time of it. I made eye contact with one of them who brought the cigarette over and offered it to me.

I said to him, knowing he wouldn't understand, 'I don't care how good it is, my lips will not be touching it.' Then I just shook my head.

He put his hands in the prayer position, the smoke stuck in his mouth, and bowed his head, then took it back to his mates, all still giggling like little girls.

Trains were now running on the line, mainly at night, and so far had not attracted the attention of the US Air Force. The trains coming from Thailand were full of Jap soldiers and armaments and going back to Thailand empty. There was a buzz that we were going there. One day all our sick were brought out and that night they were put on a train for Thailand. There was a lot of talk in the camp about how the bridges had been sabotaged by the POWs building them. I was hoping they would hold up until we were out of this hellhole.

About a week later at morning *tenko* we were told by the senior army officer we too would be going to Thailand. All I could think was that we were being sent to do more back-breaking slave labour. One afternoon came the call, 'All men out!' We grabbed what little we had; most of my clothes had by now rotted so I was back to my G-string and boots. I was lucky – most men had no boots. The camp commandant came out to thank us for our hard work as the train rolled in. We thought he was going to give us our 'pay', as we knew it was brought up the line. He never did, he just robbed us. I had no money left and looked at Knocka's watch still on my arm and thought, if I have to.

The train was pulling steel boxcars and about 50 men were loaded into each. It was alright at night, but during the day they were like ovens. One man, delirious and overcome by heat, started calling for his mother. There was a deathly silence as we listened to him. We never even had any water for him; he died before the train stopped for wood and water. At our next stop we took him off and buried him, then convinced the guards to leave the door open. It gave us two things: cool air and a view.

The scariest parts of the trip for us were going up the mountains and ravines at walking pace, and going down even slower. But the native train drivers knew what they were doing; the bridges, built with wood and bamboo, all by hand, swayed from side to side, but they didn't fall. With thoughts of the rumoured sabotage fresh in my mind we crossed into Thailand. I thought how easy we had it on the Burmese side of the line; I couldn't imagine how hard it must have been for the men who'd had to build the line around the mountains and the bridges, all by hand. It was a slow trip. One morning we woke to the sight of the Thai lowlands. Thank God, we've made it, I thought. To where, I didn't know yet.

Passing camps along the way we noticed they had vegetable gardens; some had pig and chook sheds. A few men with slouch hats would wave to us as we rattled past. They were beautiful days; we passed many temples, green rice paddies as far as the eye could see, row upon row of different fruit trees, and elephants working with logs. I was starting to feel good about where we were going.

The train came to a shuddering halt. The drivers were good at going up and down mountains, but on the lowlands passenger comfort was not considered, or maybe that was just their way of saying goodbye. There was a large group of Allied officers and men there to greet us. You could tell the difference; the officers still had reasonable uniforms. The men, slouch-hatted, were in rags. There were about 300 of us, most just wearing G-strings.

'It's good here, old mates,' one said as we slowly crawled out of our boxcar. Anything had to be better than the train.

The men helped us out. One, holding my arm, whispered, 'Don't worry, mate, we know what it's like.'

'Are there any navy blokes here?' I asked.

'Yes,' he answered, 'there's quite a few.'

That filled me with anticipation at catching up with my old mates. 'How far is the camp?' I asked.

'About half a mile,' he answered.

We marched to the camp and had our name, rank and official number recorded, then were taken to a stream where I had my first wash in five days, no showers here. At least we had soap. I was then given a new G-string, a shirt and blanket.

We were taken to the mess hall where they put on a great meal for us, beef stew and vegetables with rice.

I was accompanied by one of the POWs, who told me, 'The food is like this all the time, and we get one egg every week plus fresh fruit every other day.'

I was back in civilisation. 'How many men are here?' I asked him.

'Over 3000. There are three camps: One, Two and Three.'

'What's the name of this place?' I asked my cobber.

He replied, 'This is Camp Number One, Kanchanaburi. You will find your mates in Camp Three; they run it like a ship with their own kitchen. They'll send someone over soon to collect you.'

I couldn't wait to get on board.

After lunch a chief petty officer I recognised from *Perth* appeared and, along with some Pommy sailors, we were taken by truck to Camp Number Three, where another reception committee was waiting for us. Everything seemed different.

A commander who I had been told was sunk early in the war spoke to us. He explained the situation in a comforting voice. 'Men, I do understand what you have been through. At the moment there is nothing that we can do about the situation. This war is not going to go on forever; hopefully we are nearing the end. In your camp you will find the food much better than up the line and your barracks won't get flooded; we have been here for one wet season. We have a hospital here and any bad cases will go to another hospital down the line called Nakhon Pathom. This camp is called Tamarkan. We all do our share in this camp. There are two watches, port and starboard. We work one day on and one day off. If you can cook you can work in the galley; if not you will work as required. Are there any questions?'

One Pommy asked, 'Sir, is there any chance of mail?'

The commander shook his head. 'Sorry, men, we keep being told different stories. One good one is that they are holding all our mail and Red Cross parcels in a warehouse in Singapore. Or that they were on a ship that was sunk by a British submarine. You take your pick,' he said.

I asked him if he knew where Leading Stoker Grieve was.

He said, 'I'm not sure. I think he is up at Nakhon Pathom. I'll let you know.'

I thought, well, he must be pretty sick.

'Alright, men, the chief will show you to your quarters.'

The barracks were very clean, but no different to the army ones in Camp One. We still didn't have any showers, but instead of a stream we had a river. We kept to our routine of not drinking any unboiled water and washing our own dixies and mugs. The chief told us what watches we would be in. He said, 'The camp has a canteen if you have any money. If not you will have to wait for the Jap pay day.'

'Chief,' I said, 'when we left Burma we had a lot of pay owed to us. Is there any chance we might get it?'

He smiled before saying, 'Sorry, mate.'

I just looked down at Knocka's watch again.

'When and if you want to, on your day off you can go outside camp on work parties. The work is not too hard and you get paid for it; it's also a chance to get out of here for the day.' He winked at us. 'Some blokes even have Thai girlfriends out there.'

I couldn't remember the last time I had any sexual urge.

Later in the day I took a walk through the camp, catching up with old mates from the *Perth*. One bloke who I knew would make it was there: Blood Bancroft. It was good to see familiar faces; there were over 300 of us from the *Perth* in this camp. I got to the canteen but there wasn't that much for sale, mainly cigarettes and tinned fruit, plus a few second-hand clothing items. I offered Knocka's watch for exchange but the canteen operator just shook his head and pulled out a basket full of watches.

'The trader will only take money now, sorry, mate.'

That night I asked some of my mates about the work parties and was told, 'After breakfast go to the bulletin board. You won't have much trouble getting on one.'

Next minute the lights went out and I could hear the Japs shouting. I didn't know what was going on when Blood Bancroft grabbed me by the arm. 'Come with me, Stoker.' He led me running outside when the anti-aircraft guns started firing at planes overhead. The buildings were pretty flimsy and were likely to be targets. The raid must have gone on for at least twenty minutes before it suddenly stopped and the Japs started shouting again.

'What was that all about?' I asked Blood.

'The only thing the Japs hit is us down here,' he told me. 'They fire straight up in the air and never hit any planes, but we cop it when the shrapnel comes back down. They won't let us build any slit trenches. You'll soon learn the routine.'

Next morning after breakfast I went to the bulletin board, where men were already milling around. I was selected for a work party with a mixture of army and navy blokes. Our job was to chop down trees and cut them into lengths for the trains. Talking with the army blokes who had worked on the line from the Thai side, I found out that many men had been killed in accidents while building bridges over raging streams and rivers, plus around the mountains that we'd passed over on the way here. One bloke said he was surprised any trains made it at all with all the sabotage they did.

I told them about the Burmese side, how we never really lost men to accident, just sickness and starvation. We had a Korean guard who was pretty good with us. After we had filled our quota he allowed us to go for a swim in the nearby river. One afternoon the guard fell into the river fully booted and spurred, plus he couldn't swim. As the current swept him away one of the army blokes dived in and managed to get him back to the river bank. He was ever so thankful and reached into his pocket and gave the bloke who saved him the equivalent of sixpence.

'We said, "Toss him back."

'In a dry voice the life saver just said, "That's all he's worth." But if we went back to camp without him we would have been in for it.'

The war must have been going bad for the Japs, as they had taken to bashing us. On one work detail, after we filled our quota, the Korean guard allowed us to go to a nearby village where they gave us bananas, as many as we wanted. I also swapped Knocka's watch for a dozen eggs. The villager thought he got a good deal and so did I. Smuggling them back into camp was relatively easy, and that night I exchanged the eggs for tinned fruit and cigarettes. I was back in business. Later in the evening I had the biggest surprise of all, and for the first time in a long while I shed tears when Slim turned up. I danced around with him in my excitement, and the first thing I asked was if he knew if George was alive.

'Yes, Stoker, he's alive. He's at Nakhon Pathom, the hospital further down the line. He's had dysentery but is on the mend and should be back here soon.'

All the stars were lining up for me and I allowed myself to think that the nightmare was finally over. Slim gave me some US dollars and French cigarettes, which were the first I had had since I had seen him at Camp Three. I lay down on my bed and lit one up.

'So, what are you up to, Slim?'

He looked around and said, 'I have one more trip into Burma.' I couldn't believe my ears. He went on, 'Do you remember asking me what I do?' I nodded my head. 'It all started in Java. Now, I know you don't like officers, but I am one.'

'Christ, you could have had it easy as an officer,' I said.

'No, Stoker, I'm too junior. The US doesn't have the tradition of the British; anybody can become an officer in our navy. Anyway, that's not what I want to talk to you about. Let's go back to Java. The senior officers left from *Houston* never knew what was going to happen to them, and if they were going to be executed someone had to stay alive to witness it, so I became an enlisted man. I was not that well known on board *Houston,* as we had a lot of new crew, and as radio operators we were mainly out of sight. Also, we suffered a lot of casualties. I was to play it by ear and see what eventuated, and I ran into two great Aussies who I could trust with the radio, which I must thank you for. That was the start of my journey in a journey.

'It all changed for me in Changi after a meeting with other American officers. They already knew what conditions were like on the Thai–Burma line, how there were practically no medicines and men were dying like flies. The only way medicines could be obtained was by smuggling them. I don't know how; they only told me what I had to know. The Free French were in Indochina and contact was made in Bangkok with them. Because the French and Germans were in the war together and the Japs had an alliance with the Germans, the French were allowed to keep their businesses going and lead normal lives and have access to medicines. When all the lines in the chain were set up, my job cover was to be the paymaster and I was to supply what medicines I could to the three camps on the line up to the Thai border. When I got to the border with my Jap guard, I would give him a bottle of whisky and leave the camp at night for a meeting with a Chinese man who would bring the medicines he had obtained from the French up from Bangkok. I had to sign an invoice for them, then they were split between the Thai side and the Burmese side. We called our Chinese link the miracle man; I'm sure he was well paid for it. In each camp I had to select a doctor, not necessarily the senior one, just one I thought I could trust.'

'So that's why you got me to take you to Weary's tent back at Camp Number Three?' I asked.

Slim nodded. 'A finer man you could never meet. This is my last trip. Most of the sick are at Camp Three and I will come back with them; deaths from sickness are dropping. The main problem now is our air force; the Japs refuse to let camps and trains be marked as POW or with a red cross. If you hear planes, take cover.'

I smiled at him. 'I have already found out that one.'

'This is definitely going bad for the Japs now, so be extra careful with them. I have heard of some terrible atrocities they are carrying out. Now, would you like some good news?'

With two ears open, I told him.

'There is going to be a mail delivery and Red Cross parcels are coming this week.'

'Can I start that buzz?' I asked.

'Sure, I don't see why not. There is one other thing, Stoker, and you should try to avoid this one. Pretty soon up to 1500 men from these camps are going to be selected to go to Japan by ship, and the way our submarines are knocking off the Jap ships, not too many are making it.'

Slim stood up and we shook hands. He was like a brother to me and I felt such admiration for him. 'You deserve a medal, mate,' I said.

He winked at me. 'I'll see you on the way back.'

Sure enough, by week's end we had our first mail delivery since captivity and the Red Cross parcels were handed out. Most had been pilfered by the Japs, who said that POWs had done it, which was quite believable to us. That night in our barracks you could hear a pin drop as men read and re-read letters, smelled and smelled them again, even though they were nearly two years old. I had a letter from my father and mother, who told me they knew I was alive after Rohan Rivett's broadcast from Java, and they had received my letter-gram from Changi. They said they were praying for my safe return; so was I. There was a pair of socks in my Red Cross parcel. The boots I had were unfixable and I was back to wearing sandals, so I wore the socks with them.

Men who were not sick started to get some condition back with better food and no slave labour. There was a concert on every couple of weeks, and cricket matches were held between the Australian, English and Dutch compounds. I don't know to this day where the balls and equipment came from, but the matches brought big crowds and were very competitive. The Yanks couldn't work cricket out no matter how much we tried to explain it to them. We could understand their baseball; they played games against the Japs a couple of times, which were always close. The Japs were very civil at our cricket matches and would clap when a four or six was hit. When a wicket went down they would cheer like us, only they cheered for both sides. Soccer and volleyball were also played, often interrupted by the now almost daily air raids. They never bombed us, mostly flying further into Burma, but it didn't stop the Japs opening up with their anti-aircraft guns. During the day we could see their shells bursting way below the planes; that's when we took cover from the shrapnel.

A worrying new development started every week, when about 50 of the fittest men were picked to go to Camp Number One, Kanchanaburi, the camp close to the railway line. I saw Blood Bancroft go. Camp life went on. Some men would sit around and do paintings of the camp or landscapes; some would draw portraits. Some of the Jap guards got theirs done in exchange for pencils, paper and ink. Some of the blokes even used to do watercolours using little paint sets like I remembered having as a kid.

One morning at *tenko* they were picking more men, and this time it was my turn. All the men chosen were to assemble in half an hour with their belongings to go back to Kanchanaburi, Camp Number One. We marched for about two hours back to where we'd started in Thailand, stopping at a large obelisk that had been built by the Japs, using our labour, in honour of the men who'd lost their lives on the railway. On one side the names of the United States and Britain were inscribed, on the other side Australia and Holland, with Thailand and Burma at the top. At the bottom was the Rising Sun with Japan chiselled onto it, and written underneath: *To the men who lost their lives building the Thailand Burma railway line.* We stopped for a quiet remembrance of all our mates who'd made the ultimate sacrifice for Japan's glory.

There was a welcoming party waiting for us at Kanchanaburi. Most of the army blokes had been moved and the camp was now filling up with the Java Rabble. Reunited again, it was good to catch up with mates from the *Houston* and *Perth*, but I was still unable to find out where George was. Blood Bancroft was detailed to show us to our new quarters so I asked him. He just smiled and said, 'You'll see him soon.'

Once again we had to have our name, rank and official number recorded, then we were marched to our quarters. Inside the barracks, George and I spotted each other at the same moment as he lay reading mail from home on his cot. He looked in terrible shape, still just skin and bones; dysentery does that to you.

He went to get up. 'Stay there, you silly bugger,' I said, quickly making my way over and shaking his hand.

He must have read the worried look on my face. 'Don't worry,' he said, 'just a dose of dysentery. I'm over it now. Give me a month and I'll be as fit as a fiddle. The hospital wouldn't have let me out if I wasn't cured.'

I offered him a cigarette and he knocked it back, saying the doctors at the hospital said they would kill him. I had it instead and told him that after what he had been through, nothing would kill him except old age.

He just smiled, fanning himself with the bunch of letters he had received from his wife. 'I can't wait till I get home to see her.'

Here at Kanchanaburi we had another opportunity to send a letter-gram home. I just wrote, 'See you soon. Your loving son Lloyd.' The lettergrams were not very big and were censored by the Japs.

The food was even better in this camp; the cooks had discovered some local knowledge. I had my first stir-fry with chicken and green vegetables in coconut milk.

'They must be fattening us up for something,' one wag said.

I could only think of one thing, with some dread: Japan.

There were work parties to go out on if you wanted to.

I heard a story from one work party about a French lady who loved Aussies, and I do mean 'loved'. I preferred to stay with George and catch him up on what had happened after I was sent back to the main camp with my tropical ulcers, how I ran into Daniel Baker and Freddie Fuggle, and how both had died from cholera and I helped burn them.

'Cholera was bad on this side of the line too, Stoker.'

I had been under the impression they only died from accidents on the Thai line.

'No, mate,' George said, 'they told me in hospital it was rampant this side.'

Being back together with our Java Rabble group, there was a feeling of comradeship, that I'd made it. The line had been like a mountain we'd had to climb. I couldn't foresee what was up ahead, but for now it was pure bliss not to be working it. George had made a set of draughts and a board in hospital and we spent many an hour playing. He told me the names of many *Perth* men who had perished after I had left. He said he had heard some stories of POWs, of all nationalities, who never had the fortitude, taking the easy way out and informing on men who were sabotaging the line, just for the sake of extra rations. They would remain nameless to me; I didn't want to know.

One morning we were out in the sun telling stories. A Jap guard came over and pointed in the air. High up we saw a lone reconnaissance plane and he said, 'He come lookee, lookee.

The dubious Japanese cholera check

He go back, speakee, speakee. They come bombee, bombee.' He made us laugh, but worry all the same.

The buzz about us being sent to Japan was getting more persistent; it was all over the camp. One morning at *tenko* our officers lined up with a group of Japanese officers, two dressed as doctors. One was carrying a clipboard and the other the dreaded glass rod. Each man who looked fit enough in our officers' eyes was tapped on the shoulder and their name was written down. I was picked, George was not. I was happy for him but don't remember how else I felt. All men chosen were marched away for a 'medical' where we each were given two tablets, then it was pants down, bend over and the glass rod inserted in your bum to check for cholera. About 200 Aussies were chosen along with Yanks from the *Houston* and Pommies, about 750 of us all up. We were to become known as the Japan party.

Our mate Slim turned up again and once more the three of us were together. He always had a surprise for us; this time it was Hershey bars. 'It's American chocolate – it doesn't melt like your chocolate,' he said.

I savoured every piece. The last time I'd had chocolate was in Java, which seemed another lifetime away. Slim always had up-to-date news of the war, this time telling us it looked like it would last another two years. This was not what we wanted to hear and it took the wind right out of us, especially George. I asked Slim how the line was holding up.

'It's still intact,' he said. 'They're replacing some of the bridges with steel ones shipped in from other occupied territories, one even from Java, most probably British made.'

I told Slim I had been selected for the Japan party. I wondered out loud what we would be doing in Japan.

Slim said, 'We'll be working coalmines.'

'What do you mean "we"?' I asked.

Slim brought out his slow Texan drawl. 'My work here is finished – now for Japan.'

George asked him, 'How come you know so much?' I hadn't told George what Slim had confided in me; I'd given Slim my word.

He said, 'It's just the way it is,' and left it at that.

The anniversary of the sinking of the *Perth* and *Houston* was upon us again: 1 March, Saint David's Day. It was the start of our third year in captivity. All the survivors in camp held a service to honour our dead comrades. The chaplain gave a good speech, bringing many men to tears. He encouraged us to focus on survival so we could go back home to our loved ones. For the married men it was just a sad reminder of what they were missing.

It must have been getting close to departure for the Japan party, as we had all been issued with a new shirt, shorts, a pair of socks and a G-string, plus, for the first time since the *Perth*, a brand new set of boots. We were also given a straw hat; they were really looking after us. Groups of mates sat and held going-away parties, saying goodbye to one another and promising they would catch up after the war was over. Most of us who were picked would have stayed if we had a choice. Some men volunteered to go; I couldn't figure them out. Here it was safe, the food was reasonable and bashings were at a minimum. With the amount of Allied air activity around, I thought that Singapore and Thailand would soon be retaken.

Slim shook his head, saying that General MacArthur had other plans, bypassing central Asia and going for the Philippines then to Japan. He told us MacArthur was on a mission and we were not part of his plans, though he could have saved a lot of POWs if he had been inclined to.

Slim had a small bottle of brandy and that night the three of us polished it off. We heard the sound of planes, unusual as they normally came in daylight, so we quickly went outside where we had made makeshift shelters, bugger the Japs. It was the best cracker night I had seen, with tracers and shell blasts lighting up the night sky. You could actually hear the shrapnel coming back to earth, some big pieces, some just splinters, equally dangerous. As quick as the fireworks started they stopped. In an eerie silence the camp lights came back on, and as usual, some men were lying prone on the ground; hospital orderlies would be out with stretchers for the dead and wounded. Back in our barracks men would be looking at empty bunks saying, 'Johnno bought it,' or, 'Nobby won't be going to Japan; he's lost an arm.' Death was never far away.

George reminded me about his parents, to give them a ring if I got home before him. I rattled off his parents' phone number, which for some reason was tattooed on my brain. George just said, 'Thanks, mate, you're a champion.'

'You're not so bad yourself, George.'

We had already had three false starts, where we would gather our belongings, fall in on the parade ground and wait around for a couple of hours for the call. Then we'd hear, 'All men back, one big mistake,' from the Jap guards.

Slim came to say goodbye to George. I noticed him handing George a little parcel; everything helped in here.

'All men out,' came the call.

Slim said, 'This is it, Stoker.'

I shook George's hand and said, 'I'll see you back home, mate.'

Standing waiting for our orders, I looked around the camp: the chicken coop, the vegetable patch, the smoke coming from the galley chimneys, our concert hall and even the Jap guards who were nearly civil to us. We knew from our secret radios how Japan was under constant air attack. I would have been much happier sitting the war out here.

This muster was the one; somehow the whole camp knew too as men flocked to see us off. The Japanese commandant came out to address us; he told us we were going to heaven. I thought, I'll know the difference, as I've already been to hell.

How we were to travel to Japan was anyone's guess; I was just hoping we never had to go back over the line. We were told to fill our dixies with food for our journey and return back for *tenko*. It was a sad occasion in the camp; we had all been through so much together. The whole camp turned out again for our departure. The sadness was covered by bravado as men called out the names of their favourite pubs to one another: 'See you at the Ship Inn,' or 'Have one for me at the Commercial.'

'Your first shout!' was a common cry, along with 'Tell my parents I'm coming home.'

Chapter 10

The first group of almost 500 POWs marched out of the camp towards the railway station, with voices still farewelling us in the distance. Among the Japan party there was an eerie silence. The Jap guards decided to have some fun with us on the way to the railway station, saying, 'Submarines, boom boom,' then making a ship sinking sign with their hands, thinking it was very funny. It never made us feel good but we just laughed at them. Slim was beside me as we marched; he told me there were a few senior officers in our ranks, even an Australian general. I never had a clue who they were as none had any insignia; I would find out later.

Before boarding the train there was a search by the guards for any contraband. It was rare for them to find anything, as by then we were adept at hiding stuff down trousers and under hats. The Jap guards (unlike the *kempeitai* – the military police) were pretty casual and nothing was found. After being treated relatively well by the Japs we thought maybe we would get real railway carriages, but not on your life. We were back to the steel boxes, 40 men to a car, back to the future again, with just our boiled rice for food. Once loaded on board we waited in the stifling heat; many men took their new clothes off and reverted back to the G-string. It was nightfall before we moved out, travelling all night and into the next day, before disembarking at another POW camp, this one bigger than our last at Kanchanaburi. It was full of Australian and Dutch POWs; I was starting to wonder how many Aussies there were in captivity. We were segregated from the main camp and noticed we had our Korean guards from Java back, including the vicious Dogface and the good Christian, who actually came and shook my hand.

We waited a couple of days for the rest of the Japan party to catch up with us. Slim and I took the opportunity to buy some tinned fruit from the camp canteen. The food in this camp was exceptional, even meat and vegetables. But we also knew how quickly that could change. We found out that this camp was for fattening the men up for the Japan party.

After two days our number had risen by another 250 POWs. Once more we were loaded into our steel boxes, now 50 per box, and waited till nightfall again before we heard the toot of the engines, one at the back and one at the front, before they shuddered off into the night. The Korean guards allowed us to keep the doors open, which gave us some relief from the heat. At daybreak the mountains were far in the distance behind us, which told me one thing: we wouldn't be going over the line. Even though a lot of the rickety bridges had been replaced, going over would have exposed us to more bombing from the ever increasing air raids by the US Air Force, who would have assumed us to be Jap reinforcements heading to Burma.

Once again we were in the lowlands, the train making good speed as paddy fields and pagodas flew past. The buzz was we were going to Bangkok and from there would be shipped to Japan. Slim told me about Bangkok, a large city with a big French population. 'There will be plenty of opportunities for us,' he said with a wink.

The scenery out the door was starting to change. Small villages were turning into suburbs, with canals linking them; everyone seemed to own a long, skinny type of boat. There were not too many cars on the roads, mainly carts pulled by water buffalo and the occasional working elephant.

Finally the train arrived at Bangkok, not stopping at the station but proceeding to a marshalling yard, which to us seemed quite intact despite the heavy aerial bombing we had been told was occurring. We disembarked and, with some men having recurring malaria attacks, the Japs issued us with quinine tablets. We were allowed to have showers at the water tanks used to fill the trains, and were warned by an army doctor with us about drinking the water. I was looking forward to getting on a ship, obviously suffering short-term memory loss at how bad they were. The Japs had set up a mobile kitchen for our use and gave the cooks bags of rice for us, that's all. We wondered if the Japs were up to their old tricks, pilfering and on-selling. Two Jap officers stopped a couple of Thai street vendors and spoke to them before letting them sell to us; the Japs didn't miss a trick, as the vendors then had to pay them for the privilege. A lot of the men were cashed up with Jap script, money that the Thais took. Slim and I had a meal of chicken satays – at least, that's what they said it was. We did get something for free off the vendors. Slim was able to ask them about our destination: it was not Bangkok but Saigon. I had not even heard of Saigon. This journey was to be a geography lesson for life.

We watched as Jap troop trains loaded with reinforcements and field guns lumbered out of the marshalling yards, heading up the line to Burma. A lot of the army blokes who had worked the Thai side of the line were chattering among themselves about the acts of sabotage they had performed, hoping at least one little act would bring the intended results to the hated Japs, with one man saying that a certain bridge wouldn't take that load. We all hoped it was true.

The guards started shouting and it was our turn to load up into the steel boxcars; it was as hot as an oven and we moved our malaria cases close to the open door. In the distance we could hear the boom of anti-aircraft guns and bombs dropping. We knew we had to wait for nightfall before departing. The buzzes were starting again. We had one man die from malaria before we even left the yard and the Japs took his body away. Finally we began our journey, hoping our bombers didn't get us, which was our biggest fear.

We had little idea – except 'Saigon' – where we were going and had two new Korean guards in our boxcar. They were young and decided they were going to enforce their will on us, pushing us closer together to leave more room for them near the open door and fresh air. As they slept we slowly regained some room by nudging them towards the opening. When they woke up in the morning they were very close to the edge. They never tried to sardine us again – there were nearly 50 of us and they knew without any doubt we could just get rid of them. Our biggest disincentive was retribution from the other guards, but they were not to know this.

The train stopped for water and wood. Villagers came to offer us fruit. I saw Slim talking to a white lady who turned out to be a French missionary. Other French people came, and a lot of the men played ball games with the children. For the married men with children of their own it was a mixture of sweet and sour. The French told us the train line went to a place call Phnom Penh, which was situated on a large river, and from there we would go by boat to Saigon. It was a two-day journey from Bangkok, meaning we only had one day to go. The land on the way was mainly jungle around small villages and was sparsely cultivated. Some of our blokes had been talking of escaping; after seeing the impenetrable jungles they soon changed their minds. Slim said there would be a better chance of survival escaping into a large town or city, but you would have to know somebody to hide you; the Japs had put a price on the head of anyone who tried, and there were a lot of snitches among the natives. If caught, you would lose your head to a samurai sword.

We arrived at Phnom Penh railway station around midnight. There was no one there to meet us. The Korean guards allowed us to disembark, the officers commandeering the waiting room for themselves. At least I now knew who the officers were. We men sprawled out on the platform. In the morning the Japs arrived and started barking orders at the Koreans. The Japs were not in a good mood and the Koreans passed it on; just when we thought the Koreans were getting better with us it was back to boots and rifle butts, waking men up and parading us for *tenko* and another search. God only knew why.

We were marched through the streets of Phnom Penh where men, women and children came out to watch. Some of the French people tossed little cakes to us; they must have known we were coming. The cakes were most appreciated. We couldn't help but marvel at these buildings, all built in a French style in the middle of the jungle, a slice of Europe. We marched to the docks, located on the mighty Mekong River, where all manner of boats were either tied up or at anchor on the river, which at this point was about half a mile across to the other side. After another *tenko* we were fed our boiled rice.

We slept on the docks and waited for a large river steamer to come alongside. Our journey was becoming a boys' own adventure. We were marched on board and found plenty of room there for us to lie down and relax; they even had awnings to protect us from the tropical sun. We were glad it was the dry season. The Korean guards let us be and set up their own camp up in the bow. We watched them drinking bottles of beer, which for us was a distant memory. They noticed our gaze and took great pleasure laughing and pointing at us. I suppose if our positions were reversed we would have done the same thing, only more so. We had some good laughs with the *Houston* boys over the size of rivers in our respective countries. They reckoned the Mississippi could take at least two Mekongs.

There was still camaraderie among the Java Rabble. There were a large number of vessels using the river, mainly fishing boats and a few traders who would stop at small villages dropping off passengers and goods. Saigon was a day and a night's travel away. With the cool breeze it was pure bliss for us; even our malaria cases were getting better with the help of the quinine, plus we had a couple of doctors with us who monitored them. Cruising down the river we noticed bigger towns with people, mainly on pushbikes, carrying bulky goods, all heading towards Saigon, which looked to be a sprawling city. As we got closer to the port we could see small freighters tied up alongside the wharf flying the Jap flag, but they were much too small to take over 700 men to Japan. There was minimal bomb damage to the dock area that we could see as we went alongside. The Korean guards, who had been on the grog all night, were brutal with us again, shouting, '*Speedo,*

speedo,' and bashing men who were too slow. The gangway only took so many at a time, but it didn't matter to them. The Jap officers on the wharf might have had something to do with their behaviour. Once we lined up on the wharf we had the inevitable *tenko* and search for contraband before being handed over to the Japanese army. As the Korean guards marched away we wondered if we would see them again. They had been on and off with us since Java.

The civilian population took no notice of us as we marched away with the Japs, obviously used to seeing POWs in this area. Our new camp was surrounded by factories and warehouses and not far from the wharf. We were separated into nationalities and had our own barracks, Aussies, Yanks and Pommies. Slim went with the Americans to their part of the camp and we had to fill in our next-of-kin cards before we were allowed in our barracks. Even though I was with my *Perth* mates, I felt so alone with Slim gone again.

The barracks were solidly built, even having a tiled roof. We were issued with a mosquito net, toothbrush and soap. This place was the best camp I had been in by a long shot, but we had not come this far to forget the basics: don't drink unboiled water and wash your own dixie and mug. Just in case men did forget, once again the doctors reinforced it.

There were many English POWs here and a lot came over to welcome us. They told us they had been here since war was declared and were quite happy to see the war out here.

We told them what we had been through on the line and they found it hard to believe.

One of our blokes said, 'And it was even worse than what you have been told.'

'Gorblimey,' said one Pommy.

They said it was nothing like that here. 'The work parties are good to get out of here for the day.'

They went to airfields to build blast walls for the Jap planes and worked on the roads. The wharves were the best for pilfering goods. The guards were not too bad and if you went on work parties you had access to the locals and the French ladies, who made the best cakes. The work parties also got paid. It was not much but allowed them to buy small supplements from the camp canteen.

We were also told that the work parties on the wharves were run by a group of Pommies who had been here from day one and fiercely controlled who could be on them. It turned out that no Aussies were allowed – they reckoned we would take too much and ruin it for them.

'We will see about that,' a couple of our blokes said.

The food as a POW was like being on the Big Dipper at Luna Park: one camp would be right at the top, then at our next camp it could be right down the bottom. This camp was up the top.

Our first week in camp was very social. The Pommies did their best to make us feel welcome and put on a concert for us.

As was usual at camp concerts, men dressed up as girls, and these ones were the best I had seen. They obviously had access to makeup, and a few men were heard saying, 'I wouldn't care.' As always, the Jap officers took the front-row seats and tried to make deals with the 'girls', giving them cigarettes and lollies, not unlike dirty old men. The concert was also as good as the best I have seen, and at its end the place erupted with applause.

As with other camp concerts, there were stalls set up outside to buy food and non-alcoholic drinks, all run by the Pommies. It was here that I had a cup of real coffee with cow's milk, my first in over two years, sitting at a little table and chair, like from primary school. An older distinguished-looking man came over to me and asked if he could sit down. I nodded my head. He introduced himself as the camp chaplain.

'Your name is Stoker Munro?'

'Yes, sir,' I said, wondering what this was all about.

'I'm not here to bash your head with religion. I do know what your journey has been like, son. I would just like to talk with you. Is it true you are the youngest POW among your men? I have noticed you by yourself quite a lot. Is that the way you want it?'

'Well, sir, the mates I joined the *Perth* with are all dead. We were only on board four months when we were sunk. My only other mate, George Grieve, is back in Thailand, too sick to travel. It's the Aussie way, sir, in situations like this. The other men from the crew have been through a lot together and formed close friendships. They don't need anyone else. Don't get me wrong, sir – we help each other out – but as the old saying goes, three's a crowd.'

'Were you in the Boy Scouts?' he asked.

I just looked at him and said, 'What's this all about? You've been talking with my mate Slim, haven't you?'

The chaplain smiled and nodded his head. 'He said I could trust you. The Japanese have allowed me to set up a Boy Scout troop for the local French and Vietnamese children and I need some help running it with men who have been in the Scouts. I have about 30 boys enrolled. The camp commandant was a Boy Scout in Japan before the war and is very supportive with materials I need. It would be good for you.'

'What's Slim got to do with this, sir?'

'I cannot tell you at the moment, son.'

'Well, sir, I was going to go out on work parties to earn some extra money.'

'I can pay you,' the chaplain said, 'and fix it with your senior officers. Is it a deal?'

'Okay,' I said.

'Good. Have you had any mail from home?' he asked.

'I've had one, sir, from my parents. It was eighteen months old. I suppose they don't know if I'm alive or dead.' Suddenly I started to cry, not knowing if it was his compassion for me or the thought of my parents worrying about me back home.

He patted me on the back saying, 'It's alright, son.' It was one of the rare times I had cried in two years of captivity.

'Wear shorts and a shirt. No G-string, Stoker.'

I smiled at him through my tears. 'Yes, sir.'

Next morning after *tenko* I was detailed off to be part of the chaplain's party. The chaplain introduced me to the other two men, Sid and Tosh, both Pommies.

'This is a good perk,' they said.

The chaplain lined us up, and out of camp we marched with no guard. For about two miles we marched and many people, both Asian and French, called out and waved to the chaplain. He seemed very popular. We stopped outside what could have been any scout hall in Australia except it had a Jap flag up the pole. From inside came the sound of Boy Scouts singing songs in French, and on entering we found a mixture of nationalities. An Asian Scout leader warmly welcomed the chaplain, who introduced me. The chaplain told me he (the chaplain) had been coming here for two years and was very proud of his boys. We soon got active with the boys, helping them with their projects. At lunchtime they put on a beautiful spread of Asian food and delicate French cakes.

'Wait till you see the mums,' Tosh said, smiling.

Later in the afternoon the mothers arrived to pick up their children, some even had motor cars. I watched with more than interest. The chaplain was in deep conversation with one French woman who was carrying a basket. They went out the back. I wondered what he'd been up to when he soon returned. 'That was a quickie,' I said to myself.

With all the children gone, Sid and Tosh started cleaning up the hall. The chaplain said to follow him and we walked out to the back of the hall.

He turned to me and said, 'Stoker, I have a mission for you, and it could be dangerous.'

I smiled at him and said, 'What could be more dangerous than what I've been through in the last two years?'

He opened a cupboard and brought out four boxes. 'I want you to smuggle this back into camp.'

'What is it?' I asked.

'Medicines.'

'No problem, sir.' I put a packet in each of my shorts' pockets and wrapped the rest in my turban and patted it down on my head.

'They are to be given to Doctor Richards. Do you know him?'

'No, sir, but he won't be hard to find.'

'He's army,' the chaplain said. 'Your lot are going to need these where you're going. I was told I could depend on you.'

'I'm an old hand at it by now, sir.'

True to his word, the chaplain did pay me. Back in camp I went to the officers' quarters and asked for Doctor Richards. He came out looking quizzical. 'Is there something wrong?'

'Can I talk to you outside, please, sir?'

He followed me into the darkness where I pulled the four boxes of drugs out and handed them to him. He looked at them in the moonlight and asked where they came from.

I just said, 'A friend, sir.'

'Thank you,' he said, before putting them in his pocket and going back inside.

We only went to the Scout hall once a week. Each time I brought drugs back for the doctor and a few cakes for myself. I started looking forward to Scouts day; it was such a pleasure being with the Scouts, where the only violence I saw was a fly being swatted. It was like being back home. Even being a drug mule held no fear for me. And I loved the cakes.

Each week in camp there were boxing matches, with a proper ring set up and a real referee. They had judges, some were even Japs, who enjoyed the matches. One week it was the Aussies up against the Pommies who would not allow us to work on the wharves; it turned into a grudge fight, with no quarter asked or given. Honours were even on the night but after the fights finished inside the ring there were a few outside with no gloves on. British and Australian officers were called to quieten it down. It had the potential to turn ugly.

Being so close to the docks we were once more subjected to periodic bombing from Allied aircraft. When they came we were not allowed out of our barracks. Two Japs would come, one at either end, and would enforce a no-smoking ban with clubs as big as baseball bats. We hoped the tile roof would protect us from shrapnel but knew it would be no help against a direct hit. They targeted the harbour mainly, but one night we had some near misses. We knew there was a cigarette factory nearby from its smell, and one morning after a raid we went outside and the camp was covered with cigarettes – the factory must have been hit. The Jap guards tried to stop the men from grabbing them. They never stood a chance and I joined in.

One night I was talking with Buzzer Bee, a signalman off the *Perth*. He told me the duck farm which bordered the camp would be a good source of meat if they could be caught and killed quietly. It would be easy to make a hole in the fence and entice the ducks with some rice. I loved duck and I knew how to kill them quietly, so I was in.

Buzzer said, 'We don't want to get caught, Stoker.'

'You get the duck and I will kill it,' I said.

'Tomorrow after *tenko*,' he said.

The next day I turned up with a bucket of water.

'What are you doing with that?' said Buzzer.

'Just get the duck.'

When Buzzer spread some rice inside the fence the ducks came running. He pulled the wire apart and quickly grabbed one.

'Give me the duck,' I said. Buzzer passed it over.

I grabbed it by the neck and stuck it in the bucket. It flapped its wings for a little while then expired from drowning. It was as quiet as a mouse. 'See, no squawking, it just puts them to sleep, for good.'

We got two and Buzzer took them to his mate the cook. Roast duck for tea.

A week later we knew the Japan party would soon be moving out again when the Jap medical team with their clipboards and glass rods turned up after *tenko*. For some reason known only to them they never wanted to give us much notice. That night Slim came to see me.

'This is going to be goodbye for now,' he said. 'We, I mean the Yanks, are not going with you guys. They're keeping us here for now.'

'Why?' I asked.

'Who can work the Oriental mind out?' said Slim. 'We never thought they'd bomb Pearl Harbor.' He gave me two tins of bully beef, some real money and cigarettes. 'It's been a pleasure knowing you, Stoker. We must catch up after the war. Come and visit me in Texas. I'll write you in Byron Bay if I make it.'

I told him I would wait for his letter. It never came. That was the last time I would hear or see my dear friend. After the war I wrote letters to Houston newspapers and had no replies. I did hear many stories of what might have happened to him but he was to be only one of many to disappear without a trace.

That night in bed I felt the loneliest since the night I'd had to abandon the *Perth*.

Chapter 11

The Jap commandant was at *tenko* the next morning. He wished us a good voyage and told us to get our belongings. There were about 300 of us as we lined up for the usual search for contraband. The buzz was they were looking for diaries. I suppose some men did have them but they must have been well hidden as none were ever found. It was a very emotional farewell for the two ships' companies. We had been through so much together, both in battle and captivity.

The Yanks lined up and saluted us as we marched out of camp. Down to the wharf we went, expecting to board a ship for Japan. There was a lot of talk on the way about the number of submarines that were sinking Jap shipping in the Gulf of Siam, which didn't make us feel good. Once we got to the wharf there were no ships, just the river ferry we'd come in on. Another buzz began that we were being sent to Singapore, but the old salts among us said that never made sense. One thing was certain: we were going back to Phnom Penh. We were hoping it was all just one big mistake on the Japs' part and they were sending us back to Tamarkan in Thailand. That was our destination of choice.

They had us load the ferry first with cargo. One of our men managed to break open a box which he found to be full of French cigarettes; those boxes were placed within easy reach for the journey upriver. That night as we chugged along the boxes were broken open, the wood deposited over the side and the cigarettes distributed among us, about two packets each. At least we deprived the Japs of them.

We reached Phnom Penh the next afternoon and who was standing waiting for us on the wharf but our old mates the Korean guards. After another *tenko* we were handed over to them and marched up to the railway station. The Koreans had no idea what was going on and made us just sit around. Finally a Jap officer who could speak English arrived. Our senior officer, General Varley from the Australian Army, approached him and was told that the line to Bangkok had been bombed and we had to wait while it was repaired. We were marched a short distance to a staging camp. It was surrounded with barbed wire and very close to the main part of town.

The Big Dipper was at the bottom again: boiled rice. I had a can of bully beef left and shared it with Buzzer Bee, the duck man. We managed to ask the Christian Korean about our destination. He told us Singapore, but I just didn't want to hope that was true.

Things were starting to get hard for the local French people. They would come down to our staging camp bringing fruits in season instead of little cakes and we swapped our French cigarettes with them. We heard news from them about the war in Europe. The Americans had landed in Sicily and Italy and the rest of Europe would be next. Rommel had been defeated in North Africa. It never made much sense to me at the time; I was more interested in news from back home. It sounded like MacArthur was island hopping – what about the countries? What about Singapore, Borneo, Java, Thailand, Burma?

We were told the line which had been bombed took about two days to fix; I thought it was a buzz until I heard the toot of the steam engine. After another *tenko* we were off again to the railway station where the train was waiting for us. Steel boxes again. I managed to buy a couple of boiled duck eggs at the station to supplement the rice. Off we went once more, still not sure of our destination. When the train stopped for wood and water we took the opportunity for toilet stops and quick showers. The faces of the local people told us of their misery at the hands of the Japs. The children were asking *us* for food; we learned that most of their food was taken to be sent back to Japan. Most of it actually ended up on the bottom of the ocean, thanks to the ever increasing number of American submarines. One day soon it would be us running the gauntlet as human cargo.

It was the usual train trip. Very high in the sky we could see bombers coming and going as they dropped their destructive loads. At times, on long stretches, once again the open door was our only toilet. We arrived at the Bangkok marshalling yards near the main dock area and could see much more devastation now from the bombing. The Yanks were getting better: ships lying on their sides or masts sticking out of the water; it was a good sight for us.

We had a couple of men in our steel box with recurring malaria, and when we were unloaded our doctor had a loud conversation with a Jap officer about our condition. The officer said we would have new proper railway cars for our trip to Singapore. Liar. Then I found out for sure that we would not be going back to Tamarkan when the train veered to the left to head south down through Malaya. This was the way we originally came from Singapore.

We left in the early hours of the next morning, destination Singapore, in the same boxcars. At each stop people would swarm around us begging for food and clothing. How different to eighteen months ago when the Malays would offer us nothing and in some cases spit on us. Times had changed for them – they now realised that the British were not so bad after all. Back then the marketplace had been bustling and there was an abundance of food for sale. Now there was nothing. Most of the men who had worked the fields were in labour camps, building airfields or repairing railway lines damaged by bombing. Buzzer Bee was in a steel box that had bags of rice in it too; we didn't know if it was the Japs' rice or ours. Anyway, Buzzer told me later that they managed to toss a couple of bags out of the steel box to children on the side of the railway line. Another of our malaria cases died and the Korean guards just pushed him off the train. We never forgot that.

It was a four-day journey for us from Bangkok through the countryside. We watched the Malays, now with Jap guards, busy harvesting latex from the rubber trees, which was needed for the Jap war effort.

Back to Singapore. At the main railway station we were unloaded and I looked around for the trucks that would transport us to Changi. We were all pretty excited at the prospect of better conditions and catching up with old mates. We lined up on the platform for *tenko* and the by now customary search before being marched away with new Jap guards. Once more the Korean guards had left us. Marching away I thought, it's a long way to Changi. Then came another disappointment for us. Instead of turning right to Changi we went left, down towards the dock area, where a new, huge POW camp had appeared very close to town, fully enclosed with barbed wire, which was a novelty for us. They never needed barbed wire in the jungle.

Again we were required to fill in next-of-kin forms before being taken to our barracks, which were the same as we had on the line, bamboo poles and attap for the roof. There were no walls. It was called the River Valley Camp and our allocated huts had been used by Tamils. They had even left a couple of dead bodies behind. It was a dysentery and cholera camp.

We set to work trying to clean the unhealthy mess that had been left as best we could. We fitted 250 men per barracks, and going by the number of barracks, we estimated there must be at least 7000 men in this camp alone. We could not understand why we had been brought here. We still thought we were going to Changi.

The next day I found out: most of the men here were building a huge dry dock, mainly by hand, like on the line. The men who were picked were loaded onto barges and taken away to a small island near a place called Sembawang. I spoke to other POWs who had been in camp for a while about what conditions were like at Changi now. They said there were still a lot of Aussie POWs working out of it. The food was not that crash hot but it was still considered a cushy camp.

The biggest problem in this camp was the poor food, just boiled rice. The other problem for us was one we also encountered on the line: lice and scabies. We would sit around at night like monkeys, picking them off one another. Sometimes we would sing or blokes would tell jokes, anything to stop us from thinking about the Japan trip. It was something none of us wanted to talk about. We had no idea what it would be like.

I was lucky, along with Blood Bancroft and a lot of other *Perth* boys, to be picked to work on the wharves. It was hard work but it still had a few perks. We soon got up to our old tricks, but the Jap guards had learned some too in the last two years and were catching a few of our blokes. They would be beaten and sent to work on the dry dock the Japs were building; they were desperate to have it finished and had introduced a second shift. I got caught trying to procure some bottles of whisky and was belted for that before being sent on the dockyard party. The work was much harder and on the same amount of food, which started to take its toll on us again.

I still had a few US dollars in my tin, which I was saving for a rainy day, and it seemed like it was pouring about now. We would return to the camp by barge late at night and mainly Chinese Singaporeans would come to the wire to sell their wares. I was in a very good position with my dollars and was able to purchase good fresh food each night. It really was a living city all night. We even had many prostitutes who would visit. We never had the money or health for that, but they looked good. I knew of one bloke who found a girl who could speak English. She would bring him a hot meal every second night. He told her he'd come back for her after the war, marry her and take her with him. He had a wife and three children back home.

We heard that our planes had been bombing Sumatra, which started a buzz that Java would be taken back from the Japs and Singapore would be next, with high expectations of an early release from captivity. It was only a buzz for us, but some men believed it and were hatching a plan to take over the barges and try to make it across the strait to Sumatra.

They never thought of the gunboats and had to be persuaded from committing suicide. It wasn't until they heard Sumatra had not fallen that they were appeased.

We were losing weight quickly; I was out of money and the cooking smells from the vendors would nearly drive me crazy. We were on the bottom of the Big Dipper again.

One morning at *tenko* we were addressed by our superior officer, General Varley, who had come from Tamarkan with us. He told us we were allowed to write another letter-gram home.

'What about mail, sir?' someone asked.

Another called, 'What about Red Cross parcels, sir?'

He just shook his head. 'Sorry, men. I do have some other news. We will be going to Japan soon. Today is 22 August 1944. Don't be surprised if we are in Japan within a month.' We had another medical inspection with the glass rod, which still just seemed to be an exercise in attempted humiliation. The Jap guards seemed to get a lot of amusement out of it, laughing and pointing at us, but we were so used to being degraded there was nothing left; no feelings or emotions.

A week later I was back on the wharf. We were loading blocks of raw rubber, the sort we had seen being harvested from the trees on our way down through Malaya. A few were 'accidentally' dropped into the harbour to see if they could float, but they never did. The boat we were loading was the *Rakuyo Maru*, and we were unaware that it was to be our boat to Japan. After we finished loading we were taken back to camp. We thought we were being given an early mark.

In camp there was much activity as barracks were being emptied of their occupants, who were being lined up for *tenko*. We were told to grab our belongings, report for *tenko* and fill out our next-of-kin cards again, to be collected from each man who boarded the ship.

Chapter 12

Up we marched to the docks, over 1000 men, mainly British but a lot of Aussie diggers and *Perth* survivors. The British had the forward hold and we had the aft one. We knew what to expect. We even had Korean guards again, though we only recognised a few. Down in the hold with the blocks of rubber there was squatting room only for most us. They had at least left the hatch cover open in the stifling heat. Some wondered if this rust bucket could even make it to Japan.

As men went up to use the *benjo* it was ascertained that a convoy was being assembled for the trip, comprising four transport ships all sitting low in the water with materiel and human cargo, two oil tankers and four destroyers for anti-submarine defence. When we sailed on 5 September, it was so hot in the hold that men were collapsing; if they kept us in these conditions for the whole trip there would not be many of us left for the Japan work party. The Japs knew it, and somebody would be in big trouble. We had General Varley on board and he and Doctor Richards had a meeting with the ship's captain and the Jap officer in charge of the guard. They came to an arrangement. They painted a line on the midships across: the men in the forward hold could not cross it and the same for us in the aft hold. There was to be no smoking on deck at night and anybody caught doing so would be severely dealt with. As well, only two-thirds of the men could be on deck at any one time.

During the day it was quite hot on deck too, and men scrambled for the available shade. Some men went up for the wind in their face while others preferred to stay in the hold in the daytime, where you could stretch out and enjoy the fresh air that came down the hatch. That night I teamed up with Blood Bancroft and had a game of cards with two diggers. We talked about Japan and wondered what work we would have to do. One of the army blokes reckoned that with all the bombing we would be clearing rubble. Like Slim, Blood Bancroft thought we would be working in coalmines. I still didn't like that idea too much. They looked at me for my opinion. I had no idea and said I'd prefer to work in a piggery. They all laughed.

Blood explained to them that I was the baby of the *Perth* crew.

'How old are you?' one of them asked.

I had to think. 'I will be 21 in January.'

'How long have you been a POW?'

I stared at him, trying to work it out. 'Two years and six months.'

'Christ,' he said, 'you've been in longer than me. Don't worry, son, you have your whole life ahead of you.'

'That's what keeps me going,' I said. 'These buggers are not going to beat me.' I believed every word I said. The next day I went topside to use the *benjo*. I decided to wait up there for the evening meal that our cooks were preparing on the open deck in makeshift kitchens. I watched the Japanese destroyers circle the cargo ships and oil tankers, exciting me with their turns and manoeuvres. Pity it was the wrong navy. Blood came over to me and sat down.

'Stoker,' he said, 'I've been looking around the ship for anything we can use for a raft if we cop it. There are not enough life jackets and I can't see many of us getting into those lifeboats.'

'I'll keep my eye out too,' I told him.

After our evening meal I got my blanket from the hold and decided to sleep topside. I had worked out a warm spot just above the boiler room and spread my thin blanket out on the deck. Lying down I looked up at the cloudless night sky, full of burningly bright stars. The Southern Cross stood out on the horizon. I watched as the stars shone on the calm waters, thinking what a great silhouette we would be for a submarine captain. Our officers had pleaded with the Jap captain to allow us to paint 'POW' on the ship's side but he wouldn't allow it; after nearly three years we still couldn't work out the way they thought. It was very peaceful lying down on the warm deck with a gentle breeze. I even felt clean, though I knew I wasn't. Suddenly I heard blood-curdling screams coming from the forward part of the ship. Half asleep, I quickly sat up to see about six guards driving their rifles into three cowering Pommies, blood pouring off their bayonets. It went on for a few minutes before they got other Pommy POWs to throw the bodies over the side and wash the blood away. They were only doing their duty, I suppose. We'd all been told not to smoke on the upper deck at night. But as the guards walked past me they were laughing about it. That wasn't on.

We were now near the Philippines and our convoy was joined by three more transports and three more destroyers, the two convoys becoming one around midnight. We all stood out in the clear night air for our trip down Submarine Alley, as the Japs called it. The Americans had invaded Saipan on 12 September and their submarines now used the route through here to Japan. We could tell the Japs were fair dinkum worried by their quietness and tense faces. They never spoke as they seemingly scoured the water for torpedo trails.

The Yanks must have had information about the convoy because we didn't have long to wait before the first torpedoes hit one of the escort destroyers. All hell broke loose as the convoy started to zigzag, the destroyer escorts going around in circles dropping depth charges. The guards herded us back into the hold and you could nearly hear a pin drop as we swayed from side to side while the ship held its zigzagging, depth charges going off around us. Eyes darted from person to person, all with worried looks on their faces, then someone started a slow rendition of 'Rule, Britannia!'. Men joined in till the whole hold was singing. It helped ease the tension.

After a while the destroyers stopped dropping depth charges and the convoy got back into rhythm, no more dodging and weaving. On we cruised. We were allowed back topside, and most of us *Perth* boys stuck together. I was dozing off to sleep just before daybreak when the whole night turned to day, accompanied by the sound of explosions, as the two tankers in our convoy exploded into smithereens. The ocean was on fire with burning oil. One of the destroyers going round in circles dropping depth charges suddenly exploded too; it must have been hit in the magazine as it just disappeared within a minute. That woke the whole ship up.

Men were rushing out of the holds when the first torpedo hit the *Rakuyo Maru* just in front of midships, sending a wave of water onto the men still in the hold. They were lucky – a few yards back and they would have copped it. Most of the men brought water bottles and hats and mustered on the deck. There was no panic when another torpedo hit further up near the bow, which didn't cause much damage, just left a big hole. A lot of the men had Jap-issue lifebelts, which turned out to be useless. We suffered no casualties and the ship was in no immediate danger of sinking. The Japs had a cannon on board and fired three rounds only; it must have been a signal to a designated Jap rescue ship that we had been hit. The engine had stopped and Jap sailors were winding out the davits with the lifeboats. There were about fifteen of the boats but Jap guards with rifles would not allow any POWs into them, even though there was room to take some of them. There were two lifeboats they could not launch, so after the Japs left in their boats, men got to work freeing them. Two Jap guards came bouncing up the ladder from the hold, too late for the boats. They were immediately recognised as the smoker killers; POWs soon disposed of them the same way the smokers went.

The *Rakuyo Maru* was drifting towards the burning oil tankers and the order was given by General Varley to abandon ship. Anything that could be a makeshift raft was thrown over the side. Most of the senior officers were in the two lifeboats, which had been freed and lowered into the water. A lot of *Perth* men stayed with the ship. I was waiting for daylight to find a proper raft. Blood Bancroft was with me. The fires were dying down and the ship looked like it would float for a while. I went down to the galley looking for food to take; it was half full of water but I managed to find some packets of rice biscuits. I intended to wait as long as I could, hoping the submarines would come looking for survivors, but in fact they had already scarpered to organise another attack, carried out on the convoy the next day. Another reason to stay was the destroyers still dropping depth charges, which killed a lot of men in the water. Some men swam back to the ship and were so covered in oil they could not climb the ladders. We put whatever debris we could find over the side for them.

As daylight came the full horror became apparent with more than 1200 men bobbing around in the ocean, floating away with the currents. A Jap destroyer came back and lowered two lifeboats to tow around, looking for any Japs; there were a few, but they only picked them up – not us. After they decided they had picked up most of the Jap survivors they let the empty lifeboats go. Hundreds of men swam for them. The Japs waved us goodbye.

The *Rakuyo Maru* was to stay afloat for another ten hours. I found an axe and started to chop down doors or any other wood I could find. Blood Bancroft and a few blokes had a decent-sized raft built. That afternoon another destroyer came back and cruised close to our ship while we lay doggo. It slowly cruised in the direction of the lifeboats, which by now had drifted to the horizon. We heard machine-gun fire but had no idea what happened. Blood and his mates went over the side into the ocean; it turned out it was the rubber in the hold that was keeping the ship afloat. I stayed with the ship and kept looking for drums or anything to put drinking water in, which was going to be our biggest problem.

I was with four men, two of whom were already sick. They helped me put a raft together from some doors I chopped off their hinges, then we slid it over the side. One of the army blokes jumped in the ocean and we threw a line to him. We helped the sick men down the ladder and followed. Exhausted, we just lay down on the raft. I had no clothes on, only my

The sinking of the Rakuyo Maru

sandals, and was covered in oil, and that night I was freezing. The only sound was the ocean slapping against the raft. The next morning the two sick men were dead. We slid them off the raft and picked up two more survivors. There wasn't a lot of fresh water; men with water bottles wouldn't share and had no idea how to ration it. The day was hot as hell and we could see shark fins circling and cries of 'Help me' and 'Mum, I love you' as men thrashed about and sharks pulled them from rafts. It was awful. One bloke on my raft said, 'There's only so much they can eat.'

There were other rafts around and, with the help of planks of wood, we paddled towards each other then roped the rafts together, thinking that if any planes were overhead it would be easier to spot us. No planes came. Late in the afternoon some men on the rafts started yelling and waving. There was a ship on the horizon and it steered towards us. As it got closer we could make out men lining the guard rail. It was a Jap transport. I thought, I don't care if I go back into captivity, just get me out of the ocean. They came real close to us and when they saw we were not Japs started yelling obscenities. We shouted back. Some of them must have had a bit to do with Aussies as, laughing, they shouted at us, 'Bad luck, mate,' or 'See you in Sydney.'

We just laughed, which upset them. One Jap eating an apple tossed it at me and it landed just short of the raft. I quickly jumped in to grab it. Now both I and the apple were covered in oil again. I held it up to the Jap who just watched as the ship steamed away from us. I wiped off as much oil as I could and gobbled it down.

All the men on the rafts collapsed into silence from our efforts. As night fell there came the sounds of men in delirium, some from drinking salt water, some with recurring malaria that sent them mad. They had to be let go as there was every risk their raft would capsize and take the rest of us with them. When daylight came our numbers were depleted. I had just woken up from a broken sleep and there was just me and another bloke on board when I noticed a hand come up onto the raft. Then another hand, next a big Jap head with an even bigger bayonet clenched between his teeth. He was just about ready to pull himself on board. There was only one thing for me to do. Quickly I grabbed the paddling plank and hit him right between the eyes. My army mate on the raft wouldn't believe me when I told him what happened; he wasn't watching. I showed him the Jap floating on his face. Then he did. The Jap was joining the hundreds of other floating corpses.

Some men, mainly Pommies on the other rafts, were slitting the veins of dead men and drinking their blood; they might have known something we didn't. I never tried it and don't know if it worked. We just lay around on our raft wondering how far it was to China. Suddenly we heard a man shouting. Thinking it was another delirious case I took no notice till I heard splashing and looked up to see the biggest shark I have ever seen with a man in his jaws who looked as small as a ten-year-old boy. It sent a chill down my spine.

My army mate said, 'I'd rather kill myself.' There was a lot who did – who drowned themselves.

Three days on the rafts and the sea was starting to pick up. A decision was made to separate them to avoid one capsizing and tipping us all over. Blood Bancroft and a few other blokes transferred to my raft. They said the army blokes on theirs had been drinking salt water, and if they all went off at the same time it would capsize their raft. We had about one army canteen full of fresh water between us, and with the sea picking up the clouds were starting to gather. We knew rain would not be far away. That night, with my lips sunburned and parched, I had to resist the urge to dip my hand into the sea and ease the burning pain. It was a really dark night, which was a good omen for us. Come daylight we were excited at the overcast sky and looked for whatever we could to catch water in. This was our fourth day shipwrecked.

The seas were now really picking up, and the raft went down in the swells and up to the peaks. After a couple of hours of this we reached a peak and could not believe our eyes when we saw a submarine. We waved like mad as we went down into the bottom of the swell. We reached the peak again only to see the submarine steaming away from us. We were devastated; men openly wept. All of a sudden my army mate swung a fist, collecting me on the jaw. I was knocked off the raft, which by now was on another peak. Blood Bancroft could only watch as I floated away. I didn't know what to do, I just knew I didn't want to die alone.

I looked around and found an old ice chest half floating. I just lay down on it, like you would on a surfboard, to distribute my weight over it. I had to hold on real tight, making sure I didn't accidentally open one of the two doors. It started to rain and I opened my mouth to the life-saving torrential downpour. Just before dark I spotted a large wooden hatch, which offered a little more stability – anything had to be better than the ice chest. I decided to swim for it and pushed off in its direction. I was a good swimmer but every time I'd get close to it, down it went in the trough and away from me. After nearly an hour it was getting dark and I thought about the big shark I had seen. I made one last try, using the waves to surf towards it. Exhausted, I finally reached it and hung on till I managed to pull my body on board and tie myself to it. There were empty water containers on it and the continuing rain slowly filled them. The dawn came with ever-rising seas; I thought it must be a typhoon. My throat was so sore; I must have swallowed oil and salt water on my swim yesterday. This was my fifth day and I wondered how long my luck would last. It had been five days since I had last eaten, except for the apple and rice biscuits I'd got from the *Rakuyo Maru*'s galley. At least I was coming from a low base.

I saw a bloke holding on to a lifesaving float as he drifted towards me. I helped him onto my raft, which then went further under the water. We spent another night on the raft, hardly speaking to one another. I was drifting in and out of consciousness. Suddenly I heard shouting and looked up, thinking I was hallucinating when I saw a submarine. I waved my arm and saw a man dive over the side of the submarine. The waves were really big now. Then, after about ten minutes, the fittest man I had seen in a long time climbed on board my raft. I started crying.

He gently patted my head and said, in a Yank accent, 'You're safe now, mate.'

He undid the ropes I had tying me on and wrapped another one around me. Together we slipped off the raft and were pulled back to the submarine. I thought to myself, if there are miracles then this is one. I could hear other Yank voices calling out. It wasn't a dream. I could still see bodies floating everywhere. Yank sailors, with tears in their eyes at the sight of me, manoeuvred us back on board the submarine. They wrapped me in blankets and gently lowered me down the hatch to eager hands. I was still crying and said to the captain, 'God bless you, sir.'

'You're alright now, buddy,' one Yank said, as the swimmer went back to get my Pommy mate.

Using spirits they gently wiped my oil-caked body as clean as they could. They had already picked up other POWs and by now knew what was required after radioing their base doctors for instructions. As the Yanks continued to wipe oil off me another one lifted my head and gently spoon-fed me from a mug of chicken soup. My lips were swollen and sore, but I grabbed the mug off him and gobbled it down. The first words they heard from me were, 'Have you got any bloody more?'

'He's an Aussie!' they roared out, clapping, and quickly brought me another mug of soup. They told me the typhoon was getting too dangerous to remain on the surface so the submarine was diving. I was one of the last survivors the USS *Barb* was to pick up.

The captain of the submarine, Commander Eugene Fluckey, visited me while I was still being fixed up, the medic now putting cream on my newly clean body. He asked me who I was.

'Stoker Munro, sir, off HMAS *Perth*, sir.' I could see in his expression that I must have looked a wreck. 'Thank you for rescuing me, sir,' I said.

With that tears welled up in his eyes. 'It's the least I can do, son.' He then asked me how old I was.

'What year is it, sir?'

'1944.'

'Well, sir, I am twenty years of age. Not too bad for twenty, eh, sir?'

Looking at me, all skin and bones, he just shook his head. 'You will be well looked after now, son.' I looked around at the other Yanks. There was not a dry eye in the place.

Two sailors helped me onto a bunk. I pushed down on it and smelt the clean sheets. It was my first decent bed in nearly three years. There'd been no sheets or pillows when I was in hospital before; just bamboo slats. I wanted to enjoy the experience, but to sleep in safety was what my body needed right then. I don't know how long I slept but when I woke up I could smell fresh bread. Two sailors who were assigned to me as carers were waiting for me to wake up. I thought I was dreaming.

They took me to the showers and gave me a good wash. Looking at myself in the mirror, I didn't recognise the stranger I saw there with long hair and goatee beard. They gave me a clean US Navy uniform to wear and a pair of slippers, then took me to the cafeteria. The other survivors they'd picked up were there but they never even looked up as they demolished the plates of food in front of them. My carers sat me down and placed a loaf of fresh bread in front of me. A knife was quickly produced and a tin of butter, Aussie butter. They cut a thick slice of bread for me and I put on a heap of it. I wanted to savour it slowly but the physical urge took over and I quickly gobbled it down. Next a huge bowl of soup was produced. I had no manners as I slurped it down too. Then it was ice-cream. When I was full my carers took me to the barber shop; yes, they do have them on submarines. I was starting to feel human again and even fell asleep in the barber's chair. When I woke up they had left a pencil-thin moustache in a wispy blond streak above my lip. It was the first time I had smiled to myself from genuinely deep down in a long time. I left it on till I returned to Australia. In the US Navy you cannot have a full beard, but in the Australian Navy the only facial hair allowed is a full beard, no moustaches.

Sleep became a big part of my life in the coming days. No more *tenko*, no more *speedo*, no more Japs. I asked one of my minders where we were heading for. He told me the Mariana Islands, to a place called Saipan.

'It's our home base. We lost a lot of our guys taking it over from the Japs.'

'How is the war going?' I asked him.

He just shook his head, saying, 'I don't know how they keep going with the amount of shipping we are sinking and the constant bombing of Japan. The ships just keep coming and we keep sinking them. The closer to Japan we get the harder they fight. They commit suicide instead of surrendering.'

'I owe you blokes a beer when we get into port. What about Europe?' I asked. 'Have the Germans been beaten? I know we invaded Italy.'

'How do you know that?' the Yank asked.

'We had secret radios and used to listen to the BBC. Actually, I never listened, but we were told.'

He shook his head again in wonderment. 'Well, we invaded France earlier this year. The Germans are fighting hard at the moment. They have to fight on two fronts, one against the Russians, the other against the Allies. We are told the fighting is nearly over in Germany. It shouldn't be long before Mr Hitler is finished, then all our resources will be directed towards Japan.'

The seas were getting bigger and the submarine was starting to get tossed around underwater. A lot of the crew were becoming seasick but none of us survivors, either army or navy, were affected. I think our stomachs had been starved for so long they would not give anything back. The commander of the *Barb* decided to take her deeper. I was in the control room at the time and he asked me if I wanted a quick look at the periscope.

'Too right,' I said. Squinting my eyes against the rubber pads I noticed the conning tower of another submarine. I didn't know if it was a Jap or what. I took my eyes off the periscope and saw their smiling faces before I could speak.

The officer of the watch said, 'It's USS *Queenfish*.'

'She's one of ours, I know that much,' I said.

They all laughed. 'She's going back to Saipan with us. There are a few of your mates on her too.' I wondered who else was as lucky as me.

Yanks do not wear shorts. We were issued standard navy dungarees and needed belts to hold them up on our skinny frames.

'Don't worry, guys,' one of the Yanks said. 'It won't take longer than a couple of weeks on Saipan to fatten you up. You will have steaks and fries, chicken and beer.'

Stuff I had only been dreaming of for the last few years. With that, my thoughts turned to home. How would we get there and how long would it take? It was good meeting these young, fresh and professional men, though they were totally devastated that their actions had resulted in the deaths of over 900 POWs. It was war, but it was also a cross that they would carry with them all their lives. I just loved them for their actions afterwards and their heartfelt remorse about something that was not their fault. If the Japs had allowed us to paint 'POW' on the side of the *Rakuyo Maru* they would not have been put in that position.

Entering the calm waters of the Saipan lagoon, us survivors were allowed topside of the USS *Barb*. My first impression was of paradise, but a closer look at the countryside showed a blackened landscape, with no trees in sight. Tanks and trucks sat at odd angles, all burned out and wrecked, and smashed landing craft lay scattered on the beach. A cleared area was full of small white crosses. Cannon fire could be heard in the far distance and US Air Force planes were landing at a far-off airfield. The *Barb* slowly manoeuvred alongside the wharf where other submarines were moored next to a submarine tender. Dockside a small navy band was playing 'Waltzing Matilda'. A line of ambulances were parked and the big brass were there too.

We said our goodbyes to the lined-up crew of USS *Barb*, the last being Commander Eugene Fluckey, each of us shaking his hand. The crew of the *Barb* had passed the hat around and gathered all the money they had on board. Each survivor was given a share from the captain as we made our way dockside on shaky legs, where a US admiral made a short speech to us. We were treated like film stars. As the admiral said, our journey of enslavement and barbarity was over. It brought tears to the eyes of the waiting crowd. To us survivors it was the start of our freedom and life, just like being reborn.

With a medic on either side of us we were led away to the waiting ambulances and transported to the base hospital. There, all eighteen of us got our biggest surprise: American female nurses were waiting to lead us inside the hospital for full medicals. The ulcers on my leg had become infected again and needed proper attention.

Slowly our frail bodies started responding to the excellent food and medical care. We were allowed to wander around the other wards, and I was told that there were other *Perth* survivors there. I couldn't believe my eyes when I saw Blood Bancroft, with his striking red hair cut into a US Navy crew cut, sitting on the edge of his bed. I never in a million years expected to see him again when I left the raft. We gave each other a big hug and I asked him if the bloke who knocked me off had made it.

Blood just looked at me and said, 'No, mate.'

I told him, 'Let's not talk about it again.'

When the hospital staff realised there were four of us *Perth* survivors – Blood, Jack Houghton, Bob Collins and me – they put us together in the same ward. All the nurses around were such a distraction for us: look but don't touch. Our bodies may not have recovered fully but we still had our wits.

We were in hospital for two weeks and after our discharge we were not allowed out of base. There were still pockets of Japanese soldiers on the island and fresh marines were being brought in to clear them out. I was amazed at the number of B-29 bombers that lined the Aslito airfield, which we were told were carrying out attacks on the Japanese mainland, only 1044 miles from Saipan. We spent our time watching movies and newsreels, mostly American. I was still hungry for any news from home. Us *Perth* survivors had a meeting with American intelligence officers about our captivity, any Japanese names we could remember and where we had been on our journey. They were particularly interested in the ill-fated *Houston*. I just sat back and let the others do the talking and they made no mention of Slim; I didn't even know his name other than 'Slim'. He was very secretive about his work with the Free French underground network. Maybe after the war it came out; I only heard little snippets of information about what they did. I remembered what Slim told me, not to talk about it, so I never did.

We had a surprise, a USO concert held on Saipan with a Hollywood movie star being the main attraction. Betty Hutton put on a great show, even singling us Aussies out for a special mention. Besides us four navy men, there were eighteen Aussie diggers, also survivors from the *Rakuyo Maru*. But our war was still not over and on a couple of nights we had to dive into foxholes when Japanese bombers came to attack the airfield.

The war in the Pacific had moved further north towards Japan. Supplies were coming from Hawaii instead of Australia and there were not many planes or ships sailing south. As there were still Japs on Saipan, the troopship *Alcoa Polaris* had brought fresh marines up from the Solomon Islands and would return to pick up wounded US soldiers in the Solomons to take them back to Hawaii. It was an unexpected bonus for us and it solved a dilemma for the Yanks: how were we going to get back home?

On the day of our departure from Saipan, at the beginning of October, once again there was a band, the admiral, submariners and nurses – most of the nurses sobbing and waving handkerchiefs. Obviously some of our blokes had made an impression. We were dressed the same as American sailors and given a pocket full of US dollars each. The canteen on board the *Alcoa Polaris* was as big as one floor of the David Jones store in Sydney. We were treated like royalty and given the best seats at the movies on board ship. During the day, apart from a few 'abandon ship' drills, we were free to do whatever we liked. I spent a lot of time playing cards and talking with the Army diggers. I couldn't help feeling a little guilty when I knew so many of our *Perth* shipmates were still suffering from deprivation in their squalid camps.

One night the captain invited us four *Perth* survivors to dine at his table. The biggest surprise to me from that was not once did we have to talk about being a POW or the *Perth* sinking; it was all about where we were from and our aspirations for after the war. When I told him I was from Byron Bay, the captain surprised me by saying, 'I know the lighthouse there. Many a time I have sailed past it, the most easterly point of your wonderful country.' He made me feel so proud of my humble little town. After dinner he produced a bottle of whisky, not having any himself but offering us as much as we liked. It was empty when we left.

Before the night was over the captain showed us a cable he had received from naval headquarters in Canberra stating we were not to talk to anybody, especially reporters, about our time in captivity as POWs.

How different it was for me on this ship as big as a passenger liner. We had the freedom to do what we liked. My time on ships so far was either down in the engine room or stuck in the holds of rust buckets with hundreds of other men. Having time on our hands we talked a lot about what we had been through during the last two and a half years and the friends we had lost. We knew full well the consequences our story could have on those still in POW camps. If we did tell journalists what we had been through and the Japs inflicted reprisals on them it would be too much to bear, so we made a vow that unless it was sanctioned by higher ups we would not talk about it to anyone.

The malaria I contracted as a POW returned, so I was back in the sick bay on the *Alcoa Polaris* for a few days on our way to the Solomon Islands and I found out that practically the whole crew knew about our ordeal. On a ship it was pretty hard for our story to remain a secret when there were 22 Australian POWs on board among the American crew and soldiers. Our story spread like wildfire.

Chapter 13

Arriving in the Solomons about 10 October, the captain came and wished us well on our journey home, and friends we made on board also came to say goodbye. The ship lay at anchor as we made our way down the gangway to a landing craft that ferried us to the wharf. We were all dressed as US sailors, our soldiers included, which the Yanks thought was so funny. Again there was a welcoming party for us on the wharf, including a couple of Australian journalists. The Yanks kept them away and led us to a line of jeeps that whisked us off to our quarters, where we filled in more next-of-kin cards. I was told that beer was good for malaria, so that night at the enlisted men's club, for the first time in years, we had good old Aussie beers. The Yanks treated us like heroes, but to us they were the heroes. Apart from a couple of the diggers, we were now in pretty good physical condition; it was just our heads that were still coming to terms with surviving when so many others hadn't.

By now our only problem was how we were going to get home from here; we hoped that a plane might be able to take us. We were so near but so far from home, and the married men were very anxious. One night we were drinking with some crew members of the USS *Monadnock*, a minesweeper; next day we were informed that their captain had volunteered to ferry us home. We were cheering.

The crew of the minesweeper could not do enough for us; I even kept a few watches down in the engine room just to break up the boredom. One night I was in the wheelhouse when a Brisbane radio station was picked up on the ship's radio; the sound of the announcer made us all laugh. I was thinking, now I know why the Yanks say we sound different. To us it was more. It was home.

The idea of it all was making it hard for me to sleep. One morning before sunrise I was up on deck and I swear I could smell home. The smell of gum trees, wattles and banksias; after all, it was the start of summer. It was very cloudy and just on daybreak the clouds parted, as if by the hand of God, and the sun was rising on the horizon. My eyes strained to catch a glimpse of the coastline as the USS *Monadnock* steered towards Moreton Bay. For about five minutes the only sounds were the thumping of the engines, the fluttering of the ship's battle ensign and squawking seagulls. I thanked myself for never giving up on survival.

By now most of the other POWs were on deck, shouting with excitement the names of pubs they were going to frequent once ashore in Brisbane. They reminded me of the promise I made to Leading Stoker George Grieve from Zillmere, a

Brisbane suburb. I don't know how but I still remembered his parents' phone number; at least I had good news for them, that he was safe in Tamarkan POW camp in Thailand, which was a pretty cushy camp compared to the line. He would be able to just sit the war out; I was certain it would put their minds at ease.

Slowly the minesweeper entered Moreton Bay. Fishing boats were going about their normal business but, to me, today was anything but normal. My body was buzzing inside with excitement. It must have been the same for the other blokes too as a quietness suddenly overcame us.

A pilot boat came alongside and a senior Royal Australian Navy officer came on board. Blood Bancroft, Jack Houghton and Bob Collins knew him; he was the executive officer on HMAS *Perth* before I joined it. The four of us were called up to the minesweeper's captain's cabin where Blood introduced me to Commander Reid.

He shook my hand. 'Pleased to meet you, Stoker Munro,' he said.

It was the first time I had ever shaken a navy officer's hand and it was not to be the last. He started asking so many questions, so many names, and again I just sat back and let the others do the talking. Some of the names I knew, a lot I'd never heard of. We could hear the shudder of the engines as the minesweeper manoeuvred alongside the wharf.

Commander Reid said, 'You had better go on deck.'

I was expecting to see crowds of people and the newsreel cameras. Instead there was an army band, senior officers and General Blamey, who later gave a short speech, but no families. We were given very little time to say our goodbyes to our army cobbers, with whom we had endured so much, as they were marched off to waiting trucks and taken into seclusion in an unused convent, where they were kept for three weeks' debriefing. Later I was told it was just like being a POW again, except a local brewery donated a keg of beer each day to them. Us four navy blokes said our goodbyes to the captain and crew of the USS *Monadnock* and promised to have drinks with them before they sailed, a promise we were not able to keep.

We were taken to HMAS *Moreton* naval base by car with our few belongings, all courtesy of the US Navy, where we were escorted to the captain's office. I thought of the last time I was escorted into an Australian Navy captain's presence; it was Hec Waller. This time it was much different. There were about five officers there in full uniform while we were still in our US uniforms. The captain's secretary sat in the corner ready to take notes so I knew we would be up for more questions. We were given cups of tea.

They started by introducing themselves to us then the captain read us the cable we had already heard via the captain of the *Alcoa Polaris*. The captain emphasised that it was up to the government to decide what to tell the population, not us.

Then we each had to read and sign the Official Secrets Act. Then the questions kicked off, starting with, 'How did the *Perth* sink?' I thought to myself, Christ almighty, she just had too many holes in her, but I never said anything. The other three blokes had been in the navy a lot longer than me so I just kept quiet. A question I could answer was about Captain Waller. I told them what I saw from the main deck, how I looked up and saw him standing on the port wing deck when a salvo of shells crashed down on him.

'But did you see him dead?'

'No, sir,' I answered, 'but I never saw him alive either.'

The other blokes remembered the names of some sadistic guards. They also asked about the conditions we worked under on the line; no amount of words could describe it unless you were actually there. They asked about so many names, if we knew they were dead. We told them some but others we could not in all honesty say, as we just never knew. The questioning was like being back there again with some memories I was trying to forget. The cups of tea kept coming and so did the questions. Poor old Jack Houghton was a married man and knew his wife was only half an hour away in Wynnum Manly.

'What was your accommodation like on the line?'

I nearly burst out laughing when Blood Bancroft said, 'Wet or dry season, sir?'

That stumped them for a minute till one officer said in a tense voice, 'Both.'

Another officer said, 'The food must have been alright, you four look in tiptop condition.'

We just looked at one another and smiled.

'What's so funny?' the captain asked.

Blood Bancroft answered for us all. 'Sir, for the last three years the main item on our menu was rice, boiled rice twice daily, while we toiled on the railway line from twelve to sixteen hours a day, seven days a week. Most of us were ill from malaria or tropical ulcers, and we had no senior officers to speak for us, as they were all in main administration camps. We had to look after ourselves, except for our doctors, who did a sterling job with what little they had. On the line the only meat I had was from the water buffalo that Stoker Munro and Leading Stoker Grieve stole one night, going out of camp at great risk to their lives. Sure, we look alright now, and that is all because of the Yanks, who smothered us with food and kindness ever since we were picked up in the sea. Yes, we look fit enough now, sir, but you should have seen us two months ago.'

That quietened the room down, and they told us we could go and have stand easy. Outside in the beautiful, peaceful sunshine we puffed on our cigarettes, not even bothering to talk about what was going on inside. Understandably, Jack Houghton just wanted to see his wife. A WRAN approached us looking distressed and asked us if we knew what had happened to her husband, Vic Duncan, who was on the *Perth*.

We just looked at one another and shook our heads, mindful of the Official Secrets Act. We knew he was on the *Rakuyo Maru* but was not with us survivors; we just didn't know his fate at the time. We thought he must have perished along with 900 other men. After the war we found out he had in fact been picked up by a Jap destroyer and taken to Japan. He survived the war.

We finished our stand easy and were told to report to the sick bay where we were to have a full medical. We were back in the Royal Australian Navy. There were two doctors and five sick-berth attendants waiting for us. When they saw the scars from the tropical ulcers on my leg they wanted to know how they were treated. I told them that each night when we came back to camp from the line, our doctors used a sharpened spoon or a piece of bamboo to spoon out the dead flesh. One of the doctors was incredulous and asked if it hurt.

I just looked at him and said, 'What do you think?'

The other doctor told me that they had a new drug for infections called penicillin. That was one of the many changes that had occurred in the three years of our captivity, as we were soon to discover. We were all declared fit to go home on leave.

We were sent back to the captain's office, still in our US Navy uniforms, where they told us we each had three months' leave. I asked the captain if it would be okay if I rang Leading Stoker George Grieve's parents. He asked for their phone number and said he would ring them for me and would let me know. He pressed a button on his desk and in walked a chief petty officer. The captain told the chief to look after us.

Before we left, the captain said to me, 'Stoker Munro, get rid of that ridiculous moustache.' That's when I knew the navy was back in charge.

The chief petty officer took us out and went straight to the pay office where we were each given 50 pounds, then had our photos taken for new identification cards. A navy car was provided to take Jack Houghton home. Months later when I saw Jack again he told me that when he got home there was no one there; the house was locked so he just pottered around in the front yard. He saw a lady walking down the road carrying groceries – it was his wife. His wife told him she wondered as she walked down the street what a Yank sailor was doing at her home. True love.

Blood, Bob and I were taken to the clothing store and issued with new Australian Navy uniforms. I got rid of the moustache. Back in uniform, I was told by the CPO that the captain had rung George's parents and they had invited the three of us home for a baked dinner that night. The captain had organised a navy car for us. I was excited, as George had done so much for me.

Blood Bancroft was to go home to Perth the next day by plane, and Bob Collins and I would be going home by train the next night. For us it was all happening so fast and we were not going to have time for our promised piss-up with the crew of the USS *Monadnock* and our army survivor mates. I wrote them a letter, sure in the belief they were having a good spot of shore leave in Brisbane. (After the war was over we had a reunion with our army mates; we had plenty of stories to retell. It turned out the army boys had to wait another three weeks before they were given leave. Thank God we were navy.)

Driving through Brisbane, we were amazed at how much the city had grown. Yank marines and sailors were everywhere, most with Australian women on their arms. The driver of the navy car knew his way around and soon we pulled up outside a home in a quiet street of Zillmere where George's parents were waiting on the porch for us. We got out of the car and the driver told us he would be back at 10.30 for us. It was a warm summer's night. Neighbours had come out knowing George was in the navy and thinking it was him coming home, but there was no George with us.

George's father looked like him only older. Tears filled both his parents' eyes as I introduced myself then Blood Bancroft and Bob Collins. We went inside where George's father poured cold beers for us and toasted our safe return. He told us the captain of HMAS *Moreton* had told him and his wife what questions they could ask of us, but they just didn't seem to matter much anymore, he said, looking at his wife who was dabbing at her eyes with a handkerchief.

'He's alright,' I blurted out. 'He is in a good, safe camp in Tamarkan, Thailand, where he just has to sit the war out. He will be home soon; he wanted me to tell you to let his wife, Kathleen, know he will be home soon.'

By now Mrs Grieve was sobbing quietly.

Mr Grieve took a telegram out of his pocket. 'I got this yesterday.' He passed it to me. It read:

It is with deep regret that the Naval Board wishes to inform you that Leading Stoker Ronald 'George' Grieve was killed by friendly fire when US Air Force bombers were conducting air raids near Tamarkan Prisoner of War Camp.

I felt sick and passed it to Blood and Bob. After all the deaths I had witnessed, George's death was the most personal. Mrs Grieve left the lounge room. It was so quiet.

Mr Grieve poured more beers for us and I said to him, 'You can't blame the Yanks. When we were there, more shrapnel from the Japanese anti-aircraft guns landed on the camp than bombs. The Japs wouldn't let us build any shelters or have markers denoting us as a POW camp.'

They all looked at me; first night out and I had already broken the Secrets Act. It was a lesson for me, to keep my mouth shut.

The smell of roast lamb came with a call from Mrs Grieve that dinner was ready. As we ate, Mr Grieve filled us in as best as he could on what had been happening at home while we were away, from the Melbourne Cup to football and cricket. Blood asked him if he knew anything about the Australian Rules in Perth, especially his beloved Subiaco side.

'Sorry, son, you'll have to wait till you get home. We don't hear much from Perth.'

We talked about everything but the war, and half past ten came quickly. Mr and Mrs Grieve came out to see us off and Mrs Grieve gave each of us a big hug. I shook Mr Grieve's hand and he said, 'Keep in touch, son.' I promised I would and I did.

We drove back in silence. The next day we were told that our parents had been informed we would be coming home. Blood left on an RAAF plane for Western Australia. Bob Collins and I expected to get our train that night but there was a muck-up in the bookings and we had another day to wait. We decided to go into town for a beer and maybe go to the pictures. There was one picture on that the papers said was very good called *Gone with the Wind*, starring Clark Gable. The theatre had a 'full house' sign up so we decided to skip it. We went to a pub in Fortitude Valley where we got into Australian Saturday afternoon pub culture. One radio had the horseracing on, with blokes running around putting on bets with the SP bookie; another radio had the rugby league match of the day on. Bob and I both agreed it was great to be home. At 6pm the pub shut and we were told we could continue out the back, but we decided instead to find a place to sit down and have a meal. There was a club up the road from the pub with a line of Yanks with their Aussie girls outside. That never bothered us at all, unaware of the trouble that had been going on in Brisbane between Aussie servicemen and the Yanks over girls. When we got to the entrance the doorman told us we were not allowed in. We told him all we wanted was a feed.

'That's what they all say, now piss off.' We couldn't believe it.

Bob said, 'We're not going nowhere, mate.'

I was right behind him when two coppers appeared out of nowhere, grabbed each of us by the arm and said, 'You two blokes are causing trouble, come with us.'

What annoyed me the most at that point was the attitude of the Aussie girls with the Yanks, who said, 'See you later, sailors,' in a condescending way. It made my blood boil.

The coppers yanked our arms and said, 'Do you want the easy way out or the hard way?'

Bob, who was much older than me, just said, 'Don't worry, we'll go.'

We stopped and bought a pie each, got a taxi and went back to HMAS *Moreton*. We never wanted nor did we expect to have any trouble; we had three months' leave to spend with family and friends, that was good enough for us. We went to the Junior Ratings Bar at *Moreton* and there told the driver who had taken us to George's house what had happened at the nightclub.

He smiled at us and said, 'I will tell you a story about the "Battle of Brisbane" which started all this animosity between Aussies, our girls and the Yanks. Our boys, all drunk one night, had enough of these Yanks who had smarter uniforms, more pay and treated women much better than we did. It was all brought to a head when Yank MPs with their big sticks got stuck into a couple of our boys. By then there was a couple of hundred Aussies. More MPs turned up with shotguns; some panicked and fired, killing and wounding some of our blokes. The wash-up of it all was our camps were moved away from Brisbane, leaving Brisbane and our girls to the Yanks, and in some cases our wives too.' I couldn't believe it. 'That's why they treated you like they did, in a nutshell.'

Next day we packed our kitbags and the captain came and said his goodbyes to us. A car took us to Roma Street railway station where we had our tickets checked and bags put in the guard's van. Bob was going all the way to Sydney and I had to get off at Casino to catch the mail train to Byron Bay. We had plenty of time to wait for the train and decided to have a few beers in the Railway Bar, which was full of Australian soldiers going home on leave, many recovering from war wounds. We were the only two sailors in a room of khaki. We were quickly served by a beautiful and friendly young lass. As she put the beers down she said to me, 'My brothers are in the navy.' She told me their names, which I couldn't remember, but they were serving together on the HMAS *Shropshire* and she asked if I knew them. I hadn't even heard of HMAS *Shropshire* myself; it came to the RAN in 1942 as a replacement for HMAS *Canberra*, which was a sister ship. *Canberra* was sunk in 1942, and we were prisoners of war by then.

'Sorry, love, I don't know them.'

She was busy and thankfully asked us no more questions.

One of the diggers came over and asked for a light. 'You mates going on leave, eh?' We just nodded our heads as he went back to his mates.

I asked Bob if he had heard of the *Shropshire*, but he just shook his head, saying, 'There's going to be a lot of things we don't know about, Stoker.'

The diggers were starting to get a little drunk and asked us more questions, questions we could not or would not answer. We were in brand-new uniforms with no ship's name on our tally bands, just HMAS. We watched as they spoke together looking over at us, by now convinced that we must have been deserters or shirkers who had been caught and were being sent south. There was nothing we could say or do. We could understand their feelings towards us and knew what it must have been like for them fighting the Japs in the island jungles. Lucky for us two military police came in; we finished our beers and decided to go outside and wait on the platform.

I went and bought myself a newspaper and a *Pix* magazine for the journey; there was a bar on the train that I thought would be full of the soldiers, so it would be better if I just stayed in my seat. Walking back from the newsagent I noticed the two military police talking to Bob. They asked me if I had my ID card. Looking at Bob I pulled it out and gave it to them. Bob then told them to ring up the captain at HMAS *Moreton* if they liked.

'We just might do that,' and they walked away after handing my ID back.

Reading the newspaper and the *Pix* magazine, we realised how much Australia had changed just by the ads and the pictures of girls in swimsuits. We were busy showing each other items we were reading when the two military police came back to us. What are they up to now, I thought.

They stood in front of us and I swear I could see a tear in one's eye. They said, 'Welcome home, boys. You'll have no trouble at all on this ride home.' They then shook both of our hands.

As they walked away Bob winked at me, saying, 'They must have rung the captain. At least we never had to breach the Secrets Act.'

We boarded the train and the military police were on it; they must have checked on us every half hour. Bob asked me how I felt, and there were two trains of thought in my mind. I was excited to see my parents, relatives and the friends I had grown up with again, but I knew I had changed so much in the past three years, and there were friends I would never see

'Welcome home, Lloyd Munro'

again who lay in graves scattered along the trail or lying deep below the sea.

This journey was much different to my last train ride, with its comfortable seats, sit-down toilets and unarmed guards. The section through the Border Ranges through forests and over narrow, rickety bridges brought memories flooding back of the line going into Thailand and of our labour, still so fresh in my mind. I had to close my eyes till we got down to Kyogle and the flat plains. Nearing the railway station the two army MPs came to shake my hand again and told me to enjoy my leave.

Casino railway station was where Bob Collins and I were to part company. There were no tears, just a 'see you later on'. I collected my kitbag and waved him goodbye for now.

The mail train to Byron Bay was on time, and the reality of going home finally hit me. I tossed my kitbag on board and stood near the door, looking at all the sights, remembering the doubts I'd had of whether I would ever see them again. I also remembered my will to survive shutting those doubts out of my mind.

The train came out of the last tunnel and on a beautiful summer's day the sight of Byron Bay was before me. As we pulled slowly into the railway station, I saw a crowd of people, the local town band and the Boy Scouts on the platform and my father's taxicab parked nearby. A man standing behind me said, 'There must be someone important on this train.'

I just smiled at him and thought about the Official Secrets Act. Then I saw my parents, Mum with a handkerchief in her hand. As our eyes met she started waving it. The train stopped and the band struck up 'Auld Lang Syne'. I was in no doubt it was requested by my father to celebrate our Scottish Presbyterian heritage. People started clapping and shouting my name, treating me like a hero. To me I was anything but, just a survivor. I placed my kitbag on the station platform and my mother came forward and took me in her arms, tears streaming down her face, saying, 'Thank God, he answered my prayers.'

I could hear voices saying, 'God, doesn't he look old.' I was only twenty years old.

Dad shook my hand. 'Welcome home, son,' he said. I noticed a tear in his eye, knowing full well he had been through the same thing in World War I.

A lot of people – my Scout leader, people I had worked with, the local publican – all wanted to shake my hand and chat with me. One thing became apparent: there were not too many friends my age here, they were still fighting the war. Thinking of them I started to feel guilty, and my thoughts also turned to the person I owed the most to for this homecoming, my Yank mate Slim, who looked after me with his canny way of turning up at the right time with parcels of food. But most of all he gave me the belief in myself that I could and would survive. I hoped to catch up with him after the war. I was glad they had no big party for me. I just wanted to go home with Mum and Dad, which we did.

The following Saturday the story of our remarkable journey on the *Rakuyo Maru* was front-page news in all the national capital cities. When the acting prime minister got up in parliament and announced to the nation a list of atrocities that our POWs had been subjected to, including the starvation diets, the beatings, slave work conditions and lack of medical supplies, which all contributed to so many deaths, the Australian people were appalled, and rightly so.

I didn't know how they got my address or phone number, but once the story appeared in the newspapers families with loved ones still in prison camps started to write and phone, begging me for any information I could give them about their loved ones. If I did know they were dead I could not bring myself to tell them, so I took the easy way out and hid behind the Official Secrets Act I had signed. On reflection, maybe I should have told them.

One morning at home I was sleeping late, and I woke to my father shaking me: 'Wake up, son, wake up.' I did, in a lather of sweat; memories filled my head, memories I wanted no part of. Dad said to me, 'We have to have a talk, son.'

That afternoon we went for a drive in his taxi up to the lighthouse. We got out and walked to a bench where we could watch the ocean. He tapped his wooden leg. 'You know I lost this in the war in France. When I came home my father brought me up here and told me to talk to him about my war. I told him everything. I told him what it was like in the trenches, the mud, the broken bodies of my comrades, the massive artillery bombardments, the time in hospital. About when they were debating whether they were going to take my leg off, and I cried and begged them not to. It brought the war back to me. He then told me to shut it out of my mind and to get on with my life. 'It worked for me, son, and now I would like you to do the same with me, for your own sake.'

But as much as I wanted to I could not. It was too fresh in my mind; there was just so much that I didn't want to put it on anybody, even my father. My way of thinking was he didn't need to know what his first son had had to endure. He'd suffered enough in his life; I didn't want him to carry my sufferings too. I decided then and there not to talk about my journey, to anyone.

Christmas 1944 in Byron Bay was a happy time for my family and friends as we celebrated with lunch together, but it was times like these that I just wanted over as quick as possible. It's hard to explain to anybody how I was feeling. Ella Speer was the daughter of our neighbours and I had watched her grow up. She was so kind to me, waiting on me hand and foot, but at the time kindness was the last thing I wanted; I was just too young to understand the difference between that and feeling sorry for me. It was like I could not recognise their love for what it was.

Complete strangers on Christmas holidays in Byron were asking locals where I lived, and they would come to my home to beg for any news I had of their loved ones in POW camps. They must have thought there was only one camp, but they were in every country in South-East Asia. I finally stopped going to the door whenever I heard a knock. My mother was my rock; she would tell them I was in Lismore or Ballina, anywhere but Byron Bay. She protected me.

I had my twenty-first birthday at home. My father presented me with a new watch; he never asked what had happened to my last one and I didn't volunteer the story. It got to the point when I had to get out of Byron, and I was pleased when my leave was up. A crowd of family and friends saw me off at the railway station second time around. It was late January 1945 and I was off to HMAS *Cerberus* in Victoria, not as a recruit but as an old salt. I had already made the decision to stay in the RAN after war's end. There were seven months left before the Americans were to drop their atom bombs on Hiroshima and Nagasaki. I had never heard of an atom bomb at this point, but the whole world was about to.

I arrived in Melbourne and caught the leave train to HMAS *Cerberus*, which had its own railway line into the depot. After completing my draft in I stowed my gear in the stokers' quarters and went to the Junior Sailors Club for a few beers, which was a hive of activity. I ran into a couple of mates who I did my original stoker's course with; they were both kellick stokers (the navy equivalent to a corporal) by now. They just sat and stared at me, looking dumbfounded, as I made my way over to their table, then both jumped up and grabbed an arm each, spilling my beer.

They started talking together, one saying, 'I thought you went down with the *Perth*,' the other saying, 'I thought you were a POW.'

'Sit down, you silly buggers,' I said. 'Now, listen to me. I'm not allowed to say much but I will tell you this and I don't want it spread all over the place. I was a POW but I'm back now. You might have read a bit about it before Christmas in the newspapers. Well, I was one of those blokes. I had to sign the Official Secrets Act, so if you blokes talk about me I will be in trouble, okay?' They both nodded their heads. 'Now, tell me, what has your war been like?'

'We've been luckier than you, Stoker. When the *Perth* and *Houston* left Tanjung Priok we were supposed to sail with you, but after the air raid we weren't able to refuel and were sent south on HMAS *Hobart* to Fremantle then Sydney. Otherwise we would have been in the same position as you. We sailed on Anzac Day from Sydney and were in the Coral Sea Battle. Later we were attacked by Jap bombers three times in one day – fortunately they missed us – and then a fourth time by three Yank bombers who mistook us for Japs. They were as bad with their aim as the Japs, thank God. Then we were at the landings at Guadalcanal; afterwards we copped a torpedo from a Jap submarine. It put a huge hole in the side and blew both port-side propellers off and caused heaps of other damage. We've been in Cockatoo dockyards ever since. We're in Melbourne for a couple of weeks to do this course in firefighting. We leave for Cockatoo and *Hobart* next week. Then we should be back to war soon. The buzz is we will be heading north for the Japan invasion.'

I just looked at them and said, 'I wish I was sailing with you.'

'Don't worry, Stoker, you've done enough already.'

My first week back in the navy proper I reported to the marine engineering school where the chief stoker told me I was to have a refresher course, which would not start for two weeks. Till then I was to muster with the spare hands at the bosun's store from the following morning.

The next day, Thursday, 1 March, was also the third anniversary of the *Perth* being sunk. I lined up with the other spare hands. My name was called out with about ten others and the chief bosun said, 'Alright, you lot, draw yourselves a shovel each – you're going to work on the depot railway line.'

I couldn't believe my ears. Before I could even think I just blurted out, 'Like bloody hell I am.'

The other sailors just looked at me. The chief bosun went red in the face and said, 'Did you say what I think you said?' Before I could answer he barked, 'You're on Captain's Report.'

I rolled my eyes and thought, not again.

Postscript

The captain of HMAS *Cerberus* at the time was Commodore HB Farncomb, CB, DSO, RVO, Navy Cross, LOM, who'd spent the previous five years constantly in action on British and Australian warships. Being privy to Stoker Munro's service record, he called the chief bosun and Stoker to his office and informed the chief that Stoker was not to be put on Captain's Report. Commodore Farncomb explained about Stoker's time on the Thai–Burma Railway and why he had spoken as he did.

'I had no idea, sir,' the bosun said.

'That's alright, Chief, you were not to know. Stoker Munro will not be a spare hand anymore. I am going to make him my driver – that is, if you have a licence, Munro.'

Stoker told the captain about his dad being a cabbie in Byron Bay, saying, 'He taught me to drive from a very young age.'

'That settles it, Chief. Stoker Munro is my cabbie.'

Stoker, true to his word, signed on for another nine years in the RAN. After completing his refresher course as a stoker he was posted to HMAS *Warrnambool*, which was on deployment in the Solomon Islands on mine clearing. It was all old territory for Stoker. When they had shore leave in Honiara, Stoker went off by himself to try to find his old quarters. He had no luck; it had all been reclaimed by the jungle.

The *Warrnambool* returned to Australia and was engaged in mine clearing in the Great Barrier Reef. Stoker was on watch on 13 September 1947 when the ship hit a mine and was sunk, with the loss of four men. It was the only Australian ship to be lost to a mine in war or peacetime.

Once again Stoker was entitled to survivors' leave, which he took and returned to Byron Bay. His father was worried about him and tried to talk him into leaving the navy, even offering to buy him a cab. Stoker declined with just one sentence: 'Dad, I love the navy.'

On completion of his leave he was posted to the newest and most glamorous ship in the RAN, HMAS *Bataan*. It was built at Cockatoo Island dockyards in Sydney and commissioned by Jean MacArthur, wife of General MacArthur. Named after the infamous death march in the Philippines out of respect to the US servicemen who participated in it, HMAS *Bataan* never saw action in World War II but was present in Tokyo Bay for the official surrender ceremonies.

Stoker finally arrived in Japan on HMAS *Bataan*'s second deployment, where the ship served with the Allied occupation force. Stoker worked ashore as a truck driver and, even though he had suffered under the Japanese, he somehow found it in his heart not to hate them and was appalled at the conditions in which they had to live. When the British departed from the occupation force, they left behind a warehouse full of clothing. Always on the lookout for a deal, Stoker, with a couple of his mates, loaded the clothing onto trucks and took it to the Red Cross centre for distribution to homeless men.

While serving on HMAS *Bataan* in 1950 on its way to Japan for a second deployment as part of the occupation force, Stoker suddenly found himself off to war again. When hostilities broke out in Korea, HMAS *Bataan* was diverted to take part in blockading, patrolling, escorting aircraft carriers and bombarding shore targets. The ship spent eleven months in operational waters before returning to Australia.

In 1954 Stoker bought himself a lottery ticket and won the first prize of one thousand pounds, a fortune by today's standards. He was going to leave the navy and return to civvy life in Byron Bay but had a change of mind and returned for another twelve years.

He served on HMAS *Tobruk* for four years then was promoted to petty officer stoker and served on HMAS *Snipe*, a navy minesweeper. On being promoted to chief petty officer, Stoker spent his remaining years on HMAS *Melbourne*, the fleet aircraft carrier, till he finally left the RAN in December 1966 and returned to his beloved Byron Bay.

After the war, Stoker unsuccessfully tried to find out what had become of his old mate Slim, even writing to the Houston newspapers. The only rumour he heard about Slim's last months in captivity was that he disappeared with other POWs from the camp in Saigon as the war was nearing the end, never to be seen or heard from again.

Stoker kept in touch with some of the submariners from the USS *Barb*. The captain of the *Barb*, Eugene Fluckey, who retired from the US Navy as a rear admiral, wrote a book called *Thunder Below!* in 1992 about his experiences as commander of the *Barb* and sent Stoker a signed copy.

There seems to be a marked difference between how the Americans recognised and decorated their heroes and how the Australians did. The captain of the USS *Houston*, Captain Albert Harold Rooks, received the Congressional Medal of Honor posthumously for his part in the Battle of Sunda Strait. Captain Eugene Fluckey was awarded the Medal of Honor for his actions in sinking the greatest amount of enemy shipping tonnage and also for his part in rescuing POWs.

Captain 'Hard Over' Hec Waller of HMAS *Perth* fought a far superior Japanese force for nearly 24 hours, saving many of his ship's crew in the action, and it was only when they were out of ammunition that Japanese destroyers were able to get close enough to torpedo his ship. After his gallant action he was mentioned in dispatches. It was not only a slap in the face for the skipper but for the whole crew.

One of the last things Stoker said to me was that death was at the start of his journey and death was at the end. There was no time to feel sorry for yourself or your mates – it was just the way it was. To survive you had to suppress all feeling, good or bad, except the will to survive.

Bibliography

A Bancroft and RG Roberts, *The Mikado's Guests: A Story of Japanese Captivity*, Patersons Press Publications, Perth, 1945

Mike Carlton, *Cruiser: The Life and Loss of HMAS* Perth *and her Crew*, William Heinemann, Sydney, 2010

Sue Ebury, *Weary: The Life of Sir Edward Dunlop*, Penguin, Ringwood, 1995

Deputy Prime Minister Frank Forde's speech to parliament, *Courier-Mail,* Brisbane, 18 November 1944, pp 1, 2

Eugene B Fluckey, *Thunder Below!*, University of Illinois Press, Urbana, 1992

JKW Mathieson, Chaplain RAN, private diary, courtesy of Naval Museum, HMAS *Cerberus*

Rohan Rivett, *Behind Bamboo*, Angus & Robertson, Sydney, 1946

Also

National Archives of Australia, Canberra

RAN Service Records, Melbourne

USO (United Service Organizations) USA, October 1944

Acknowledgements

I would like to express my thanks to some wonderful people who helped in the writing of this book. To Tim Harris for his friendship and encouragement, Sarah Brehaut for her typing and Dianne Martin for her meticulous editing. To my good friend Len Collins, a well-known artist in the Northern Rivers of New South Wales, for his true-to-life sketches of the POWs' journeys. To Ella Lucas, nee Speers, for sharing her memories of Stoker from when they were growing up together in Byron Bay. And last but not least, to researcher Trevor Pleace, my old mate.

About the author

David Spiteri was raised in the Western Suburbs of Sydney where he was happier learning about motorbikes than 'reading, writing and 'rithmetic'. After leaving school at Year 10, he joined the Royal Australian Navy where, for many of his 20 years of service, he worked as a chef. His mixed cultural heritage – Maltese and Australian – no doubt led to his appreciation of cuisine.

His first book, *The Prez*, reflects his lifelong passion for motorbikes and motorbike clubs.

This book, *Stoker Munro Survivor*, grew from his years of service on HMAS *Perth* and his interest in the history of the first *Perth*.

David lives in the Northern Rivers area of New South Wales, where he tends his small property and enjoys cooking for family and friends at weekends.